BEYOND THE LABEL

MAUREEN CHIQUET

Beyond the Label

Women, Leadership, and Success on Our Own Terms

HARPER
BUSINESS   *An Imprint of* HarperCollins*Publishers*

Author's Note:

Names and identifying details of many individuals have been changed to protect their privacy. I have tried to recreate events, locales, and conversations from my memories of them; however, time and distance may have created slight variations in the details of each and every situation and conversation.

FIRST EDITION

Designed by Bonni Leon-Berman

Library of Congress Cataloging-in-Publication Data has been applied for.
ISBN 978-0-06-265570-7

17 18 19 20 21   LSC   10 9 8 7 6 5 4 3 2 1

To my life's most precious partners:
Antoine, Pauline, Mimi, and Tess

CONTENTS

INTRODUCTION

Just keep following the heartlines on your hand.
—"HEARTLINES," FLORENCE AND THE MACHINE

S hortly after I left my position as chief executive officer of Chanel, I had a panic attack. I had decided to clean out my closet and store my impressive assortment of Chanel jackets, bags, and shoes in the basement. It was a psychological and metaphorical purging of sorts, meant to make room for a new identity. Besides, I had worn the same uniform for nearly thirteen years—any variety, shape, color, or texture of a Chanel jacket and skinny J Brand jeans. Don't get me wrong; I'm not complaining. It's any woman's dream to slip her arms into the delicious silk-lined sleeves of a plush tweed jacket, and I fully appreciate my luck owning and wearing so many of these exquisite creations. But the same silhouettes that had once caused me to stand proudly in the mirror now felt like they belonged to someone else, to a different time in my life. Even though I had brought my own twist to the classic Chanel look—pairing even the most delicate couture jacket with torn jeans and motorcycle boots—these days I yearned to reclaim my *own* true style, inside and out.

So that explains the shock: my closet was nearly empty once

I'd packed everything away. My jeans, ribbed American Apparel tanks, and smattering of Hartford printed shirts would never be suitable for a job interview, let alone dinner in the city with friends. That's when I texted Jeffrey, an old friend and the owner of the eponymous Manhattan boutique, for help: I needed a new look.

Stripped of my usual confidence, I entered the store under the icy scrutiny of a row of pristinely dressed mannequins. Their porcelain stances seemed to mock my comparatively disheveled appearance. As if out of habit and in an attempt to reassert my style credibility, I reached out to touch the clothes and evaluate the fashions on the first set of T-stands and racks in the men's section. *See, I know what's hot,* I tried to claim. They stared back in silence.

I worked my way back past the shoe department, haphazardly picking up a silhouette or two while desperately hoping help would soon be on the way. Usually I longed to be left alone during store tours with colleagues, hoping to experience a boutique like a customer. Not this time. No one seemed to notice me so I pressed on, breathing a sigh of relief upon entering the more discreet and familiar women's section. Hiding behind the racks, I rummaged through the newest fashions pondering what might work. Holding one after another of these lovely garments before me, I tried to imagine myself wearing something so different from my daily uniform. As if by default, I kept gravitating to the fitted tweed jackets and had to force myself to sort through blouses, blazers, and even fuller-cut pants. Just as I was starting to feel like a fashion failure, Terrance, one of the store's personal shoppers, tapped my arm, warmly introduced himself, and offered to be my chaperone.

He led and I followed in a dance from one designer to the next.

"These pants are really cute but I don't really wear wide-leg silhouettes. I'm too short and they'll make me look stumpy. Besides, the waist is too high. I generally don't wear Celine. The styles are too boxy." There I went with all of my biases. My first reaction to nearly everything was at best reluctance and at worst, outright rejection; but as I look back, I wasn't really rejecting the clothes themselves, I was struggling to imagine myself taking on a new identity—and letting the old one, which had served me so well, go. Terrance nudged me to consider new looks. "Just try this one, you'll see. It looks completely different on."

The real action started in the dressing room. Arms loaded down, Terrance beckoned two other associates to help solve my fashion dilemma. Style after style, including brands I had never wanted to consider and some I had never really heard of, floated into my dressing room until every wall was festooned with a gorgeous array of shimmer, shine, texture, and color. As I tried on different outfits, the woman looking back at me in the mirror smiled broadly; I was giddy with a sense of newfound freedom to reinvent myself. It's not that I didn't love who I had been; after all, being CEO for the pinnacle of luxury, working with such talented teams, living part-time in my beloved city, Paris, and meeting wonderful artists, *had* added up to my dream job. But now it was time to shed that label and redefine myself.

I mean, let's face it: it isn't really about clothes. Leaving Chanel, I had to begin to reimagine myself entirely; I suddenly found myself the "leader" of nothing more than my own life. What would it feel like to wake up without a conference call to China or a hundred emails to answer? How would I fill up the now empty spaces on my habitually overstuffed calendar? With both of my daughters grown and away from home, I didn't even have any doctor's appointments to organize or daily advice to give. Who was I now, and who did I want to be?

It's so easy to confuse our identities with our positions, titles, or roles. And maybe they do define us for a time, along with a host of other monikers like mentor, CEO, wife, or mother. We assume and take on all sorts of different labels all the time, and it can be scary when we begin to notice that those once-comfortable suits no longer seem to fit or represent who we truly are. But I have learned that these constructs are far more fluid than they seem, whether they are foisted upon us or self-imposed. It's not simply a matter of shedding the expectations others set for us but, so often, shedding the narrow or rigid standards we've set for ourselves. Getting comfortable with the ever-changing, less definable "you" underneath the roles we play in the world takes courage, time, and a willingness to keep pushing the boundaries of your comfort zone. For me, being curious, observing with my eyes, ears, and heart wide open, immersing myself in something new, testing what speaks to my soul and continually asking myself what I care about, what I love, and why I am doing what I am doing—all of these things have helped me move beyond many labels over the course of my life.

And for you, too, there may be moments in your career or your life where you find yourself no longer the person you want to be, or in roles that no longer express enough of who you are. And like me, you will have to make a choice: accept the form you have taken on or make a change, even if it starts simply by changing into some new clothes of your own choosing.

I hate labels and boxes. Always have. Still do. Maybe it was growing up Jewish in the homogenous Midwest. Maybe it was being the first child of rather liberal parents during a particularly rebellious cultural era, or perhaps it's just that I was never really able to limit myself or anyone else to any particular category. Whatever it is, each time I've found any label imposed on me, I've eventually felt the need to shrug it off or at least push back around its edges. And I haven't been particularly fond of rigid social structures, either.

I've never gone exactly by the book, even if I've often *learned* the rules. So perhaps it's no real surprise that, at least in my own mind, my path to the "C-suite" (and the interlocking Cs of Chanel's famous logo) started not with a passion for fashion or a business degree but with goat cheese. Yep, that's right, goat cheese.

When I was sixteen, I fell madly in love with France during a month in Provence. Beauty seemed to spring forth *everywhere*, and the French seemed to possess an intuitive sense of aesthetics and design that spoke to something deep in my soul. I was captivated by the soft light caressing the limestone buildings, the fields of lavender, the vases of wildflowers adorning even the humblest of picnic tables, and, most notably, by my first encounter with goat cheese. Stinging, acrid, eye-wateringly delicious, and elegantly consumed as part of a ritual refined to reap each and every flavor, goat cheese—a far cry from its bland American cousin—blew my senses open wide.

It wasn't just beauty that the French seemed to live for and breathe in, but a kind of freedom that emboldened me to radically extend the borders of my more conservative Midwest childhood in the 1970s. At the time, French New Wave film directors were creating roles for women beyond the narrow band of American Hollywood starlets, and as an undergraduate at Yale I became enchanted by the young women in these films who had somehow escaped the pressure to conform—the same pressure I'd experienced back in Saint Louis. I longed to *be* French and live immersed in beauty, to let it pour into my senses. I had no idea where this longing might take me, but, coupled with my incorrigible determination, it no doubt set my course.

I tell you this because aside from having to contend with whatever labels may have been foisted upon *you* or that you've chosen for a time, the resounding anthem today seems to be "follow your passion." But to me, it's more than that. Allowing yourself to follow the crevices of your heart lines is a messy process and not easy to characterize or rationalize into neat and tidy lists and boxes; it's often a matter of following the whispering intuitions and inklings that defy standard categories such as college major and job title. I could never have said my passion was "goat cheese" or have known how to translate my sensory cravings into a job I loved. I could never have known that late-night conversations over scotch and soda about the "eyes" of the camera in French New Wave films would prepare me for creating desire as a marketer or feeling my way through design as a merchant. All I *really* knew was what I *felt:* an inexplicable pull toward beauty. The search for beauty led me from America's heartland through the back roads of northern France as a young sales representative with L'Oréal, then to America's Gold Coast during the go-go years at The Gap, and finally back to Paris and behind the gilded doors of the house of Chanel. I've achieved more professionally than I ever dreamed of and yet it's exactly what my heart and my instincts guided me to do. Wandering along the edges of experiences that make me slightly uneasy *is* my comfort zone. A little scared, a little uncomfortable, a little on the edge. It isn't so much thrill-seeking—it never has been—it's a fundamental curiosity that drives me.

How ironic, then, to find myself almost three decades later asked to share career advice with a new generation of women: How did you get to the top? How do you succeed in a mostly male-dominated corporate environment? How do I get a mentor? How do I get a promotion? How do I achieve work–life balance? They want answers to all of it—career, family, happiness, life. And I would like to be able to supply them, but of course I can't. I don't have *the* answers—no one really does—but I do know the kinds of attitudes and sensibilities, the questions and the curiosities, that will lead you on paths to self-discovery, beyond recognized borders and conventions, and well beyond the labels that others want to use to define you. How do you define yourself? That's up to you. I can't give you a "five easy steps" or even tell you where to do an internship, and despite my career in fashion, I can't tell you how to dress the part any more than I can tell you which roads, exactly, to take. But by revealing to you the squiggly track of my own heart lines and the lessons I've learned, I hope to encourage you to find and follow your own.

I wrote this book to start a new conversation, to open up the aperture through which we look at the world. I want us to reconsider what it means to be a woman, a mentor, a wife, a mother. I am tired of hearing about "glass ceilings" or being expected to "act like a man" (but, God forbid, don't be bossy) to get ahead. As a CEO, I discovered that even our notions of successful leadership get shimmied into the narrowest of models. I want to free the concept of leadership from its gender straitjacket, encourage you to be fiercely feminine, manfully masculine, or everything in between in accordance to what feels authentic to you. What if we recognized different strengths and honed them rather than trying to conform to another way of being? What if we changed how we measure, assess, and value leaders to include a broader range of qualities and skills? I want to help you notice the beauty of imperfection, shed light and love on your shadow, recognize that the humanity of storytelling might trump any algorithm you could invent or adopt.

My journey has been about embracing paradox in all parts of

my life. Why should we separate art from business, feelings from logic, intuition from judgment? Why can't you study literature and become a CEO? Who says the quiet introvert can't become a powerful, effective leader? Who decided you can't be determined *and* flexible, introspective *and* attuned to the world around you, wife, mother, *and* top executive? And where in the rule book does it state that standing unflinchingly in your vulnerability won't make you stronger?

I wrote this book for those of you who are tired of trying to squeeze into constrained categories, who long for integration and wholeness in everything you do, without limits on who you are or who you will become. I want to offer you some stories about critical moments in my life, when I have jumped in and immersed myself in a new identity and had to let go of everything I've known to find what will best redefine me. I want to share with you how I managed (or sometimes stumbled) through these times, and what I've learned (and continue to learn) along the way. I won't provide a set of rules or dictates, no "how to" or any bullet-pointed lessons—only a patchwork of moments, some impressions, and sparks of ideas from which I hope you can create your own narrative.

Every one of us has a unique journey. By sharing my decidedly nonlinear road map, I hope to help you find and follow your own. It's time to move beyond labels.

BEYOND THE LABEL

ONE

Breathing Deeply

Warm steam redolent of scorched rubber seeping up from under the ground. The slow screeching sigh of an arrival or departure. A dull horn signaling it's time to board before the doors shut. Most Parisians avoid the Metro grates or simply walk over them without noticing the odor, the heat, the sound of travel. I love everything about the Metro, but particularly the smell. For me, it *is* Paris—a city of contrasts and contradictions. Even today, the experience of the Metro envelops me and whispers to me that I am home. I take a big breath in and there I am again, in Paris for the first time at sixteen, ready to step outside of my Midwestern frame and take in the immense beauty of a new picture.

My parents and all of their friends adored living in Saint Louis, thanks to its superbly beautiful, well-maintained suburbs, streets lined with centenarian trees, safe schools, and high-quality cultural offerings. We lived in the suburb of Creve Coeur, considered one of those good places to raise your kids. That is, if your kids fit into the vanilla conformity of Girl Scouts, piano lessons, and gymnastics meets. That wasn't the case for me. I couldn't carry a tune to save my life, any tumbling I did was over my own two feet, and I got kicked out of Brownies.

My father, a litigation lawyer, had toured around the world as an actor after dropping out of college and came back to get serious after the sudden passing of my grandfather. (Fortunately, back then you could take an equivalency test.) When I was young, my dad started to collect wines from the regions he loved and, with the desire to sound sophisticated like him, I parroted the names of vintages from Bordeaux to Burgundy to Tuscany to Piedmont to Alsace. As I would imitate my dad, swishing the wine around in my mouth, sucking it in with a slight gargle, trying to taste the berries, earth, or honey he described more distinctly, I would create pictures in my mind of these faraway places, imagining myself there speaking with a perfect accent.

My mom searched for ways to expose us to the wonders of nature and the richness of the arts albeit close to our cozy, little world; we went to the Muny, an outdoor amphitheater, to sample musicals like *My Fair Lady* and *Guys and Dolls* while swatting mosquitoes in the sweltering summer heat. We took hikes in local wooded areas and found caves to spelunk. On occasion we might take a trip to the planetarium, where I'd follow the brightest star, hoping it might take me to a new dimension. It's not that I disliked where I lived—in many ways, I had a privileged, picture-perfect childhood—it's just that as an avid reader and dreamer, I wanted to explore a greater canvas. My mom's excursions did little to anchor me in Saint Louis, but what did pique my interest was the way my mom constantly considered things through the lens of aesthetics and beauty. By pointing out to me the subtle variations in how things looked, sounded, and felt, she began to help me develop a sensitivity and curiosity to see and discover more of the world, to break out of the first box I found myself in, Saint Louis. (Later, of course, she would come to wish that I had moved back to her beloved city after college.)

Because my appetite for learning and expanding my horizons compelled me to study hard and get good grades, my teachers considered me a "shy, good girl." I was a little withdrawn, living in my head, so classmates often labeled me snobby or aloof. In lieu of social ambitions, I often lost myself in my favorite books, movies, and TV—anything with a story. No one in 1974 believed introversion to be a good thing; it was supposed to be corrected, like crooked teeth or nearsightedness. My mom tried relentlessly to find activities to pull me out of my shell, but I shied away from team sports, clubs, singing groups, and cheerleading (unlike my younger sisters, Suzanne and Andrea, who seemed to take to my mother's encouragements far more naturally, excelling socially and athletically). I wasn't an unhappy child; I just knew that something was missing for me in pursuing the things other people seemed to want.

Being the firstborn, I felt the weight of responsibility to excel but also a little entitled to get what I wanted. Maybe it was my awkward social skills, my comparatively klutzy lack of physical ability, or just plain sibling rivalry, but I was far from the ideal big sister. Suzanne, three years younger, and I had our fair share of sisterly spats, usually spurred on by my annoyance that she was "copying me" (even if this was far from the truth). And I mostly shunned her sweet invitations to play, except right before bed when she was tired, and I would then coax her into my made-up game, where we would each invent our own fictional stories. My youngest sister, Andrea, was eight years behind me. With such a large age gap, I usually dodged the cute, blond-haired blue-eyed toddler, just wanting to go my own way without too much interference or interruption.

Until the age of fifteen, I went to the local public school where more than a few students, who came to class high and fell asleep while the lax teachers taught by rote, sold drugs in the halls. I asked my parents if I could apply to the much more challenging John Burroughs School, the only non-parochial, coed private school in town. My parents were thrilled that I came up with such an idea despite the steep tuition. Getting in wasn't quite so easy, though. I took the entrance exam with borderline results. Thankfully, after being waitlisted, a spot opened and I squeaked in.

As I climbed the stone steps to Burroughs on my first day and entered the long hallways lined with wood paneling, wearing my best hippie-chick skirt, I was confronted by students decked out in full preppie regalia: brightly colored Lacoste shirts (collar flipped, please), Lily Pulitzer pants (printed with turtles or other sea creatures), and brown Topsiders (laces untied and holes near the toes preferred). Most Burroughs students had been enrolled in the same school since kindergarten, so their social circles were fully formed. And with very few exceptions, no one else was Jewish. I fell painfully short of the norm.

One morning I arrived at school to find DIRTY JEW graffitied on my locker, which somehow felt all the more offensive as my family considered themselves "reformed" and I never had any particular emotional tie to my faith. Being Jewish just felt like part of my DNA, like having brown eyes, but I began to understand that regardless of how you consider yourself, others would invent their own definitions for you.

This type of anti-Semitism wasn't unique, though much of it wasn't overtly hateful or malicious. But it could still cause discomfort for those of us who didn't fit the standard profile. At its annual Christmas *tableau vivant*, Burroughs selected a group of beautiful students to illuminate the stage in a reenactment of the birth of Jesus. Attendance was mandatory, so the only way to get out of going was by presenting a note excusing you for religious reasons. While the event was not meant to be religious, the singular adulation of one very specific belief system bothered me. Why, for example, were we not seeing a reenactment of Judah and the Maccabees during the rededication of the Jewish Temple, commemorating Hanukkah? Or why weren't there other moments in the year where we might celebrate different but equally important cultural or religious events? Perhaps it had to do with the uniform religion of the student body. If so, it only pointed out a more significant problem. Attending felt like an impossible trade-off: participate in something I did not quite endorse or risk isolating myself even more by refusing to attend. I showed up . . . begrudgingly. My only possible recourse to avoid embarrassment and feel like I was "rebelling," however lamely, was to sit in the back with one of the other Jews in the school.

Bias takes all kinds of shapes and forms. I am sure at some point in your life you've felt this way about being "gently encouraged" (read: given no choice) to conform to something that made you uncomfortable. As an adolescent desiring to succeed, I was wary of the consequences of not fitting in and suffering the possible harsh judgment of others. Later in my career, as a woman trying to make my way through the executive ranks, I noticed that the subtler the bias was, the more insidious and alienating it might be. You may have had this experience: a colleague insinuates some kind of prejudice (be it about your gender or any other defining feature) that doesn't threaten your career or cause you any noticeable harm but makes you feel ill at ease. Since nothing illegal has occurred, any push-back or rebellion you might try only seems to prove that *you* are defensive and therefore at fault for making a mountain out of a molehill. So while this intense desire to please and an aversion to criticism served me well for many years—even helped me climb the corporate ladder—I would later discover how it was also a part of my shadow, causing me to lose a sense of who I was and what I cared about. Always playing by the rules, especially when they appear the "norm," definitely has its limits. You sometimes find yourself drowning in the swirl of public opinion and ultimately losing yourself.

❖

Despite feeling like I was swimming against the stream in these early years, I found my home in the classrooms of a few exceptional teachers who opened my eyes to new worlds and kindled my passions to experience something outside of this cushioned Saint Louis existence. One of them was the suitably named Mr. Faust, my acting teacher, whose biting wit and sarcasm and his passion for theater made him one of the coolest people I'd met by that point in my life. He inspired me to love acting—the only activity I practiced obsessively for my three years at Burroughs. Mr. Faust wheezed as he labored up the steps to the stage, script in hand. With an exaggerated flip of the wrist, he directed my acting partner to step aside. Pausing to wipe the sweat from his brow, he instructed me to read the male character's part while he took over my part. I realized that he wanted me to wander into the other character, hear what he heard, and feel the impact of those words I had just been speaking. Mr. Faust was teaching me to *listen* before speaking. This exercise pushed me way out of my comfort zone because I had single-mindedly memorized my own part and now, suddenly, I had been forced to switch sides, as it were. Even more challenging, I had to listen as Mr. Faust took on my part, imbuing it with deeper inflections than I'd been able to muster. Instead of telling me what to do, he was asking me to see and feel *myself* from another perspective, to understand how the other character might respond to my lines so I could refine my own presence. How impossible, I thought at the time. This skill required the contradictory process of both being fully inside my stage identity and observing it from another angle. Suffice it to say that this little technique—practicing self-awareness, the capacity to "switch sides" and see the world from someone else's perspective, all while enduring uncertainty and discomfort—

came in handy later in my professional life in ways both obvious and surprising, from the very first time I went on a job interview to the times I had to speak before large audiences, not to mention when I was a senior executive called upon to make strategic decisions that would affect the daily lives and careers of the people in my entire organization.

Those experiences in the theater gave me a place to try on identities of all kinds and to appreciate the value of stepping into someone else's shoes. Just because I was shy didn't mean I wasn't fascinated by people. To the contrary, my self-consciousness and timidity made me hyperaware of everyone around me. I would watch even their most minute expressions for clues about who they were and how they felt. Because I was so worried about being exposed or seen, I developed a deep curiosity about others' lives and became a keen observer of the world around me.

I found another glimmer of hope in French class. Whenever my high school French teacher, Ms. Stanley (I thought it was supercool that she used "Ms."), described the monuments of Paris and corrected our conjugation of the verbs *être* and *avoir*—both irregular, of course—her eyes sparkled. Later on I would come to appreciate that Paris itself is irregular, and perhaps that's what appealed to me: astonishingly beautiful, yet imperfect—elegant and gritty all at the same time. Massive, broad avenues and quaint, windy streets. Well-heeled men with wide-wale corduroy pants and tweed jackets on their way to work, walking hurriedly beside the flashy, blond-wigged prostitutes of Pigalle, with their torn black fishnet stockings and smeared red lipstick, staggering on their way home. This is the Paris of paradoxes with which I fell in love. In that first French class, I still didn't know much about the city or the culture beyond the lovely sound of the guttural *r*'s, but something told me—a kind of hunch, I suppose—that we were meant to meet.

It helped that my dad, whose affection and attention I always sought, spoke fluent French. He had traveled to France only twice, but his accent was flawless. He had learned the language through a unique method at his high school: no textbooks until the second year. He would just listen to the sounds, absorb them, and repeat what he heard. I became convinced that the only way to speak like a French person (and have the appreciation for all of the good cheese and wine my dad so loved) was to immerse myself wholly by living with a French family. I asked my parents if I could go for the summer.

I arrived with the other study-abroad students at Charles de Gaulle Airport. We were to spend the day in Paris before setting off for our host families scattered across the country. As I passed through the airport's narrow corridor and up the escalator, I entered another world, a different life, although I had no way of knowing then the importance of my adventure. I was just stepping into the unknown, excited and scared.

Still sleepy from the plane ride, we were herded into a bus bound for the City of Light. My nose pressed against the window as I craned my neck to take in the full height of the Arc de Triomphe. The bus drove at breakneck speed into the circle of cars as we approached the base of the monument, but before

I could soak up all of its elegance and majesty, we were zooming back out and barreling down the Champs-Élysées. I felt my heart pound, tears welling up in my eyes. There was something about the contrast—the clean, powerful architecture of the monument ringed by the frenetic, whizzing cars—that grabbed my soul and just wouldn't let go. The light broke through the clouds and shone on the gold cupola of Les Invalides. I wanted to absorb everything—the crooked cobblestone streets, the wail of the sirens, the golden glow of the earth-colored buildings, even the acrid smell of the bus driver's freshly lit Gauloises mixed with the stale wine on his breath.

Jet-lagged and weary the next day, I boarded the train to meet my host family. I was filled with trepidation. Although I had crafted a letter of introduction in my very best French several weeks earlier—my father had even corrected it—I hadn't heard back. All of the other kids in the program had these lovely correspondences going with their host families. The perfunctory but sweet postcard I finally did receive—it had apparently been lost in the mail—was signed "Dominique, Thomas, Lucas, Arthur." Was this family all men? What kind of name was Dominique? I had no idea what I was in for.

I was stationed in Provence in a town called Calvisson, actually a very small village tucked away off a *Départementale*—a windy, country road about half an hour outside of Nimes. I had a moment of utter panic as I stepped off the train and searched the crowds, trying to figure out who would be picking me up. Had they forgotten me? Finally I heard a woman calling my name, although I didn't recognize it at first because she pronounced it "Mo'r'eene," rolling the *r* and hanging onto the *n* at the end. It was more song than speech, as I later learned was common to that part of France. I spotted a woman with big round glasses, the lenses as thick as Coca-Cola bottles. She pushed through the crowd nervously, her large brown curls bouncing with the same rhythm of the sign that bore my name.

"Bienvenue! Je suis Dominique," she said. So Dominique was my homestay mother! She extended her arms to welcome me into her round figure. I leaned in for the traditional two-kiss greeting, but surprisingly Dominique's hands stayed firmly on my shoulders for an additional kiss. *"Ici, on en fait trois"* ("here we do three"), she said with a warm smile. *"On est dans le sud. On est plus chaleureux que les Parisiens"* ("We are in the South. We are warmer than the Parisians"). She swooped me up into a Citroën sedan and we headed for her home in Calvisson.

The house was one of many in a row, hidden behind brightly painted green doors punctuating the golden limestone that lined the narrow street. Pushing open the door, I discovered a small courtyard, where a table covered with a cheery colored yellow tablecloth held a vase of freshly cut wildflowers. *Les cigalles*, or cicadas, were chirping so loudly in the summer heat that I could barely hear or understand what Dominique was saying. It hardly mattered; I was exhausted and so relieved to see that there was, in fact, a host mother in my new family.

Dominique led me through the courtyard into the house. I peered into the kitchen and spied colorful vegetables—tomatoes, peppers, squash, and eggplants—brimming over an unpacked market basket. The smell of roasted rosemary reminded me it was almost time for lunch. Dominique led me to my room on the second floor, up a small stairway. "Put down your bags," Dominique told me in French. "Then we'll have a bite to eat and go to the beach." I didn't think we were near any beach, but I loved the sun and was up for an adventure. Really, at that point, I was just glad that I'd understood the word *plage*. "My sons Lucas and Arthur are already there," Dominique said. *Ah, two boys—what luck!*

Dominique and I sat down at the table in the courtyard and she poured me a cold rosé despite my age. One of the specialties of this part of France was goat cheese. My father had given me my first taste of goat cheese in Saint Louis, but what I tasted at the very end of this first meal was something quite different. There were three small, round disks on the table. The largest had a tan, wrinkled skin, the second—smaller, smoother—was rimed with gray dust, and the third, the smallest, was compact, uneven, and almost blackened. Dominique persuaded me to start with the first, the softest one, so that I could still taste the others later. "The firmer the cheese, the sharper the flavor," she explained. It seemed that there was a very precise method to eating goat cheese in France—an order to consuming and relishing each flavor. One must start with the least pungent to preserve the taste buds and allow them to gradually take in all that the sharpest cheese could offer. I had to plunge my knife forcefully into the "mildest" cheese. I then made every attempt to spread it like peanut butter onto the baguette, but the soft inside, the *mie* (what other culture has a separate word for the inside of bread?) just rolled up into little balls. I watched Dominique cut a neat, clean triangular wedge from the *crottin*, fit it snugly inside her piece of baguette, and, with almost the same motion, take a bite and a long, deep swill of wine. She sampled each cheese this way but explained that I didn't have to try the strongest one . . . yet. My mouth was already singing from the "mildest" cheese. Before I could even bring my torn-up piece of bread and cheese to my mouth, I could feel my nose tickling from the sharp odor of the ash from the aged *crottin* still on the table. But once I slid the cheese onto my tongue, I knew I would never eat the American version again. The firm and creamy texture kept my tongue scraping the roof of my mouth to savor every last bit as my taste buds exploded. I would soon learn that this ritual—*slow it down, relish it, take it in fully*—epitomized the French approach to beauty.

Soon it was time to head to the beach. I went up to my room, grabbed my swimsuit, some shorts, and a T-shirt, and rushed back to the car. The Citroën was a 2DS model, the long sleek one whose suspension system would float up once you turned on the engine, like a flying saucer ready for takeoff. And take off we did. As we traveled from the country road to the Nationale (a much faster two- to four-lane) street and then onto the Autoroute, Dominique chattered away, asking me lots of questions about my family, which I muddled my way through with monosyllabic answers. I'd thought my French was pretty good until I got there, but Dominique kept using one expression I just could not figure out:

"*mon fang.*" Did she have a toothache? And why did she mention it so often? And what did that have to do with how many brothers and sisters I had? My French-American dictionary was no help.

We were in the car far longer than I expected. Dusk was quickly approaching. I was wondering whether we would have time to take a dip once we reached the beach. I began to make out the sea in between the monstrously ugly high-rise buildings of La Grande-Motte that loomed over the shores. As we turned the corner around an enormous, pyramidal apartment building, I wondered how the same culture, so refined that it offered wide varieties of goat cheeses and fresh-cut wildflowers on a lunch table for two, could build such things. This wasn't exactly like the pictures of the French Riviera I had seen in my schoolbooks.

We parked in an overcrowded lot and walked through a sea of car campers. Dominique proudly pointed to our "caravan," a white trailer with its very own lean-to. It suddenly dawned on me that we would be spending the entire weekend—yes, the weekend—there. I had packed only a T-shirt and shorts. No toothbrush, nightgown, or even an extra pair of underwear. I awkwardly tried to explain, but suddenly Dominique threw her arms around a tall, slim, and elegant young boy. "*Voilà Arthur, ton petit frère,*" she said. He leaned over and gracefully gave me a salty, sandy three-kiss greeting with a crooked little smile. Then a shorter young man, as slim but with a chest full of hair and several days' worth of beard, came over. "*Et ce bel homme s'appelle Lucas,*" Dominique announced, beaming with pride. Lucas swept back his curly, shoulder-length hair into a quick ponytail before giving me his own scratchy three-kiss hello. These two young men were my new French brothers.

As we made our way into the cramped caravan, I tried again to explain to Dominique that I hadn't brought anything but a simple change of clothes. She finally understood and, with a laugh, reassured me that while I was in my *maillot* during the day, she would wash my clothes. With the sun's heat, they would be dry by the evening. I marveled at this nonchalance. Besides, *mon fang*, we were at the beach, and it didn't matter. The French seemed to hold these things so much more lightly than we do and, when surrounded by what they love, just make do.

Dominique's husband, Thomas, was a mechanic. The years of hard work showed in the creases of his eyes, narrow slits with just a hint of blue sparkling through them. He wore his thick hair slicked back in an almost fifties-style pompadour. Now that meeting my family was complete, I looked around the very small caravan, wondering where we all might sleep, as the back held only one queen-size bed—for Dominique and her husband, Thomas, I assumed. But when it was time to turn in later that night, I learned the boys and Thomas slept under the stars, well, beneath the lean-to, and Dominique and I would in fact share the bed. *"Mon plaisir,"* Thomas said, his heavy hand resting on my shoulder, assuring me that he would gladly give me his spot. Any dislike of sandy beds quickly fell away as exhaustion from the trip, excitement from the first meeting, and the strain to understand the singsong accent of the South pulled me down into a deep sleep next to the warm and tender body of my new French *maman*.

At the communal bathroom the next morning, it was a complete relief to step into a stall, my very own space, where I might not have to speak French for just a minute. I tilted my head up into the spray, and there, peeking over the top of the partition, was a young man, a huge smile on his face as he watched me. I let out a tremendous scream that had the advantage of chasing him away . . . fast. Unfortunately, it also created quite a ruckus in the shower complex, with lots of people yelling "*Ça va*," "*Que se passe t'il?*" "*Tout va bien?*" Feeling invaded and traumatized, I told my brothers what had happened, but neither seemed to think it was such a big deal. Sensing my own discomfort, they vowed to protect me and stand closer next time. The French had a different way of thinking about nudity. Back home, nudity and the sexuality it represented were taboo for a sixteen-year-old "good girl." It felt wrong to be exposed, to be seen, because it implied a vulnerability that felt dangerous. The French, however, seemed to think it was natural, even beautiful. Women of all shapes and sizes sunbathed topless and children frolicked nude on the beach. Nobody batted an eye. I admired the French way of accepting their bodies and aspired someday to have enough courage and confidence to be "seen" without fear of judgment.

Back home at Calvisson, I learned that Arthur, my younger brother, was a ballet dancer. He was getting ready to study at the Conservatoire de Paris for a couple of weeks. In the back of the house was a small library with double glass-paned doors. Arthur would on occasion go into the study, put on some beautiful classical music, shut the doors, and practice. I often hid behind the edge of the doorway so I could watch his fluid, elongated movements, his sweet and serene face as he followed the music. I had no idea what good ballet might look like, other than seeing *The Nutcracker* in Saint Louis, but Arthur's dancing put me into a kind of trance. Once he spied me out of the corner of his eye as I watched him. He cracked a huge smile, giggled as if he were in on the secret, too, and invited me to sit and watch. I fought back my tears as I watched his body sweep and bow across the room. Each day after that, I waited until he came home from his lesson to watch him dance. Unfortunately, he had to leave for Paris soon after. He went on to become one of Paris's Etoile dancers under Rudolf Nureyev.

The summer was filled with adventures near and far as I traveled deeper into the scenery and the tastes of French culture. We spent many lazy, hot summer days just allowing time to flow, listening to the *cigalles*, walking on the dirt paths outside of town, visiting with the neighbors, buying various groceries at different places along the way. The countryside itself was a grand adventure into sensory delight. The lavender harvest toward the end of summer perfumed each and every molecule of the air with an intoxicating aroma. The infusion went so far beyond smell, entering your very pores. Dominique often took the dried lavender and wrapped it in Provencal fabrics of pale yellows and greens, dotted with silhouettes of the *cigalles*, to keep the company of socks and other clothing in drawers.

Less aromatically pleasing, perhaps, was our trip to the goat cheese farm. Not only had I learned that there was a revered ritual for eating and savoring goat cheese but that buying it from the right person was equally important. For my caretakers, knowing a good cheese maker was a point of pride, and they considered this particular farmer to make the very best cheese in a town with a population of fewer than four thousand people. To say it was a farm was a bit of a euphemism; it was more like a rickety old shack. The cheese maker himself looked the part of an archetypal French farmer, with big, thick, swollen hands, the crevices blackened from years spent working in the fields; a deeply wrinkled, red face; and tiny lines on his cheeks and nose from years of the mornings' *ballon de rouge* (glass of red wine). I can still see the wood shack, stacked crates, and ambling goats, and smell the cheese my family purchased for our home stash. This "fine" cheese was hard as a rock, and pungent really doesn't even begin to describe the experience of taking a bite. It was almost like putting a wad of wasabi in your mouth: your eyes watered uncontrollably, your nose wrinkled in response to the unwelcomed assault, and you felt the back of your head tingle. I shivered from the attack on my mouth, wondering whether this acquired taste was reserved for the French alone.

To me, there's something vital about wandering along the edges of experiences that make me uncomfortable, letting go of all of my preconceived structures to be able to step into others. I find this to be essential to my existence; I don't know any other way. I want my explorations of life to be like learning another language. I could have learned French by looking at textbooks, memorizing words, and awkwardly stringing together sentences . . . but really learning French meant taking myself out of my own language and *assuming* the other one. It required looking at what surrounded me and no longer seeing it in terms of what I once knew. For example, if I saw an umbrella, I would try not to conjure the word "umbrella" and its corresponding translation, *parapluie*, but rather try to consider directly what the French called the object. It required listening not to the words or the grammar but to the connections between the words. It meant forgetting the language and rules that I had learned and entering an entirely different context, calling upon a new and different way of listening and expressing myself.

That summer abroad I began to understand the French through the simplest of daily ceremonies, such as *l'heure de l'apéro*—the much-revered cocktail hour. No matter how hectic the day, there's always *l'heure de l'apéro*. It's a necessary pause, a moment to sit back, reflect, talk, and play *Pétanque*. In the South of France, you will have Pastis, the licorice-flavored liquor that must be mixed with regular table water. Each evening my host family set out different types of Pastis. Nobody in Provence makes your drink or asks what you'll have. It is assumed that you will drink Pastis. Some families even produce their own. There will be a carafe of water in a bottle wrapped in a Pernod label. Long, tall glasses. Maybe one piece of ice, but never more, because the French have no use for ice. Ernest Hemingway famously wrote about what happens to Pastis when it hits water. A clear liquid when it comes out of the bottle, Pastis becomes cloudy once it combines with water. Just watching it transform itself and taking in the scent of anisette made my head spin.

L'heure de l'apéro was all about the ritual of beauty—a moment in the day before dinner to stop everything else and to just be. My family was simply taking the time to appreciate the beauty so inherent in everything around them. To the French, this gesture might be invisible because it is so much of who they are. To me, it awakened every sense I had and made me feel alive.

Even on our walks through the town, I could feel this new sensibility awakening in me. With no school, job, or friends during my stay, hot summer days held little structure in the South of France. We would sometimes simply meander through the village, nodding and greeting some of the neighbors sweeping up the stairs before the green-painted doors of their homes, and winding our way up to the top of the village on a dirt road. I was always parched, as the air was dry and the dust had been kicked up by our trek out into the open space. Most people along the way just nodded and smiled, unsure of what to say to *l'Américaine*, as Lucas had introduced me. One day we climbed to a high spot above the village so my family could show me the view. I became short of breath, not from the walk but from what was before me: there was nothing really to see, no manicured gardens or astonishing structures, no historical sites—just the view of wildflowers—red, yellow, blue poking out of long, yellow grasses. As I looked over the village, taking in the incredible beauty, absorbing it—time just stood still.

I missed my parents but was way too engaged, too excited, to feel the tug of anything else I once knew. Occasionally I'd call home, using the old French phones, which were a dull army green color with big, clunky receivers, weightier in my hand than the American counterparts I used so frequently as a typical teenager back home. Yet the dials were clean, elegant, with a beauty and simplicity so representative of French design. For the French, everything counts. Everything. Not like the Italians, who approach the decorative arts in an explicitly technical way. For the French, the sense comes from within. It comes from the earth. The Italians craft the telephone. In France, the telephone crafts itself.

When it was time to leave my summer in the South of France, I cried and so did Dominique. She didn't have any daughters, so for her to have a young girl in her life was very tender and warm, and I felt her need for feminine presence. I was incredibly sad about leaving; France had become home. I knew that everything had changed. That it was only the beginning.

When I returned home to Saint Louis, I felt displaced. It wasn't lost on me that Creve Coeur, our town, literally translated as "broken heart." Perhaps an apt description of my return. In *Mrs. Dalloway*, Virginia Woolf describes being inside her life and outside her life at the same time. That's what it felt like to be back "home." I longed to be back in France, and I craved hearing French so I could speak it again. I immediately began plotting my return.

Something broke open for me. I was taking in life more fully than I had ever done in Saint Louis. This complete immersion into another time and place, another language and culture, beckoned me in ways I could only sense but hardly express at the time. Having experiences like this began to feel like something core to my very existence. Was it France? Was it the way they slowed down and appreciated beauty? The remarkable paradoxes that allowed for a richer view of the world? Was it my newly found freedom outside of the conservative Midwest? For the longest time, I was sure it was all about everything French. Later in life, as I evolved in my career, I discovered it was something more profound—the awakening of my senses and the need to be in places where I could use them productively. In the end, France allowed me to understand the beauty in paradox—something my college studies illuminated, my work at Gap and Chanel confirmed, and that inspired a major leadership initiative near the end of my term as Chanel's CEO.

Speaking of "in the end," some twenty years later, during one of many summer vacations in the Luberon, not too far from Calvisson, I finally grasped the meaning of *mon fang*—that unfamiliar phrase I'd heard Dominique and others in the village use so often during that first visit to France. The butcher in a small shop was recounting to a customer the story of his drunken, irresponsible son as he sorted filets from rump steaks. He kept sighing and saying, "*mon fang.*"

The lightbulb finally went on. "*M'enfang*" was "*mais enfin!*" The French often elide words so that they spill together, and in Provence they substitute the Parisian sound of "eh" at the end of "enfin" with "ang," the sound of the South. The phrase means literally "but in the end," and yet its more implicit significance told me something else. "*M'enfang*" was used as a dismissive counterpoint, a soft acceptance of or a surrender to the messiness of life and its beautiful imperfections. And for me, it seemed to indicate a challenge to almost anything that might pretend to be definitive or a sort of "pure truth." It suggests that "in the end," despite what happens—all of the things we get caught up in every day, perhaps all of the traps and boxes we think we can't escape—there exists something more to the picture, something deeper, more important, almost essential, something we may have missed. What was I missing? I was on my way to finding out.

TWO

With Fresh Eyes

The musty air was suffused with ideas from the world's greatest thinkers, scholars, inventors, poets, and politicians. Floors and floors of books, so many words and concepts, all seemed to weigh down on me as I sat, confounded, at a cracked wooden desk. A single lightbulb, my only companion, dangled sullenly from a frayed cord and shivered almost imperceptibly with each sigh I made.

To avoid possible social distractions and the graying banks of snow in the middle of a New England winter, I had braved the steam tunnels (where few dared to tread alone), which ran underneath the campus of Yale University into the immense cathedral of knowledge—Sterling Memorial Library. Ducking and dodging drops of water from the blackened steam pipes lining the low ceilings and fearful of running into a wayward tunnel rat, I emerged from the subterranean system of pathways and made my way up to pray to the goddess of knowledge (depicted on the massive fresco in the nave) who guards the entrance to the infamous "stacks." Maybe *she* would know where this degree in literature might take me.

The creaking walls recited the brilliance of past students, all of whom I deemed more worthy of a place at this venerable institution. I looked around this sanctuary of worldly wisdom and wondered: Did I really belong and would I graduate with *anything* useful? Would any of this stuff ever mean something or would I be forever lost in my self-imposed, deconstructionist liturgy, murmuring incomprehensible terms like "logo-centrism," "differance," and "grammatology"?

❖

Just two years after my romance with France had begun, I headed off to college, hoping at some point—maybe during a semester abroad—to rekindle my love affair with all things French or at minimum to find out what might lie beyond the conservative straitjacket of Saint Louis. Despite my good grades, my test scores didn't compare to those of my college roommates, most of whom hailed from New York and Connecticut. They spoke an entirely different language, using a vocabulary I'd never heard, referring to places I'd never been: Horace Mann, Fieldston, Dalton, Choate, Andover, Exeter. It didn't help that my new friends loved to ask if I had indoor plumbing in Missouri or cows in my backyard. When I arrived that fall, I was certain Yale had made a mistake admitting me.

What's more, *everybody* had a talent. Not a high school, extracurricular-activity-type talent, but what seemed to me a ridiculous, child prodigy–like talent; they composed music, directed plays, and sang in ways that far exceeded any caliber I'd seen so far. With some vague hope of continuing the acting I'd been encouraged to pursue back in Mr. Faust's drama class, I managed to muster the courage for one open audition, with such disastrous results (the director whispered to his assistant during my entire monologue) that out of sheer embarrassment, I decided to forever abandon my active expression in the arts and instead focused on studying them, pulling them inside me in an entirely different way.

Which is how I found myself safely nestled in the middle of a giant auditorium during Introduction to French New Wave Cinema. I had signed up for my first college film class because it combined nearly everything I loved most: beautiful imagery, rich stories, and, of course, French. I also secretly hoped to impress some of my artsier friends whose dancing, singing, and acting I could only admire. *A kind of guilty pleasure*, I thought, knowing that I would never be able to wield a camera like Renoir, Truffaut, or Godard. The closest I might come to any great artist, I imagined, was at a random party at Studio 54. (Incidentally, my friends and I, enviably unaccompanied women, did manage on a few occasions to glide in past those infamous red velvet ropes and huddled hordes of poor souls into the very heart of the New York Art scene.)

Fortunately, I figured out how to wedge this film class neatly into my literature major by making the argument that both film and theater were, in fact, forms of text. Sound, image, music, and light constituted a moving series of signs and symbols that we, as the audience, needed to interpret, just like any piece of written work. I became fascinated with how the evolving interplay of images and words could elicit specific reactions and emotions in a viewer and how each viewer's interpretation of a film or play might be completely different.

Through a new, controversial, and, at the time, radical literary theory called deconstructionism—which challenged the idea that *absolute* meaning could exist at all—I started to understand that these reactions and emotions, and in fact *meaning itself*, came to life in a fluid co-creation between artist and viewer. The deconstructionists purported that you can never know the author's precise intent; that instead, readers (or viewers), the ever-changing sets of eyes and psyches that might be encountering a work, create their own meaning from the text (be it film or theater, for me). In film, that meant the director, actors, lighting specialists, and a host of others worked together to convey a story that we, as the audience, would interpret with our own filters. The artists and their crew might be trying to deliver a certain message or evoke certain emotions, but in the end, they can't really control how each spectator might relate to what has been created. Think about the times you've been at the movies with family or friends, and you walk away with different impressions. While you may share some ideas about what the film meant, you each experience the cues in myriad ways and no one will ever entirely know what the creators "meant." This premise, which may today seem evident, sent traditionalists in the English department into a tailspin at the time. And it rocked my world. The idea that there might not be simple "right" and "wrong" answers about constructs like plot, theme, and character—that there were, indeed, an infinite number of interpretations, and that creation wasn't a one-way street—made an indelible impression on me, one that would show up years later in how I thought about products, advertising, business strategy, and leadership. These new ideas gave me permission to examine the world with fresh eyes and to notice my own biases and bias in general.

And it wasn't just about noticing biases. French New Wave films, far less glossy and more documentary in style than their Hollywood counterparts, opened my eyes to the act of *noticing* itself, by making obvious the persistent presence of the camera. In *A Bout de Souffle* (*Breathless* in English) by Jean-Luc Godard, there are moments when you as a spectator can actually *feel* the camera blink as if it were human. The omnipresent camera puts us in the action of the film, invites us to feel what the characters might be experiencing. When the young lovers Patricia and Michel are in a taxi, the camera bounces along while we watch the back of the taxi driver's head; we see the world the way the couple might see things. Godard, in particular, uses music and sound at odd moments, sometimes even obscuring the dialogue. The hyperrealistic roar of a plane going by or the loud honk of horns might drown out the actors speaking. At first, I had no idea why these shaky cameras and random interruptions were significant. Growing up with films like *Jaws*, *Kramer vs. Kramer*, and *Star Wars*, I was accustomed to watching airtight story lines with scrubbed, retouched images. Now I was beginning to understand that these films' less polished, more natural style was asking us to open our eyes to the everyday, the banal around us, and showing us ways these things might continually influence how we experience life and interact with each other.

Through these films (and a deconstructionist "lens"), I began to take on the eye of the camera, observing things and people more keenly. I started to understand that paying close attention was important and that bias was inherent in any act of interpretation—whether watching a movie or interacting with people. My trip to France had awakened my senses, but now I could see the possibility of putting this "awakening" to use, even if I couldn't have known that this intellectual exercise would result in anything more than heady conversations over scotch and soda at the smoke-filled Anchor bar just off campus. I couldn't have known how sitting in a dark projection room in some basement on campus would impact my entire career, but I did sense that refining my ability to observe, discerning the cues that influenced how I reacted or felt about any given film, and understanding that these very same cues might mean something different for someone else, would somehow influence my future. These ponderings actually set the course for how I approached my work, my role as a leader, and even how I would choose to live my life.

In my first job after college, as a product manager at L'Oréal in France, I found myself perpetually faced with decisions and choices—everything from packaging to advertising to point-of-sale in my product category, the decidedly mundane "hair colorants." And yet it was the way of thinking I learned in those courses on film and literature that taught me the most about how to do my job well and distinctively. When I needed to choose a font, the layout of an image, or even a color for in-store signage, noticing and paying attention to each and every detail, understanding how they worked together to create meaning, seeing through a customer's eyes, and feeling what she might experience, set me apart from the other business school–educated marketers who sometimes held on too tightly to research or conventional models to assess a potential new product or campaign. It wasn't, I'd realized, about *analyzing* every detail to come up with "the right answer" (since, inevitably, the choices were unlimited). Nor was it about comparing everything to something that might have come before it. *Seeing and feeling* how the various signs and signals might be understood by a customer and embracing the notion that there were multiple ways these visual cues might affect a customer gave me a powerful method for making the most compelling choices. Over the course of my career as a merchant and a marketer, I'd see this dynamic play out again and again. Even good marketers sometimes mistakenly assumed that customers would see things exactly as they did, or worse, they rushed to categorize customers into neat and tidy segments, as if customers' decisions were always rational, emotion-free choices.

As I confronted these kinds of professional quandaries myself, I would think back on my studies in film, particularly the gritty way the handheld camera worked in French New Wave film. It seemed to stumble upon the moments in life almost as if by accident, letting us steal into a scene, eliciting our emotions. We might laugh, cry, cringe, or jump because we would feel deeply involved in what was happening on the screen, as if we were taking part in the action ourselves. The imperfections weren't smoothed out but rather were brought to life. These directors invited us to appreciate the beauty there, too. Images in those films told us stories; they painted pictures that we as viewers might understand in our own ways, and relate to our lives, usually within the context of our own emotional experiences. They appealed to something deeper than our rational minds. I began to see a parallel in the creative work at L'Oréal. Our customers would react to an image, not by finding all of the mistakes in it, analyzing it, or taking it apart, but by how it would make them feel about something in themselves, in their lives, and in their aspirations. I started to sense that tapping into these emotions would become a kind of compass for me, something that, despite my lack of experience and technical knowledge, would both direct me and anchor me along the way.

Several years later when I went to work at The Gap, I also began to appreciate the deconstructionists' view on syntax. Great scholars like Jacques Derrida argued that words meant nothing without the context of other words surrounding them; and words would easily change their definitions when surrounded by others. This "shape-shifting" seemed to apply to more than just words. I saw it work when I proposed a brand-new product for The Gap, a product that proved to be a definite "rule breaker" especially for a company that, up to that point, had sold mostly denim with a few khaki pants thrown in for good measure. Yes, I'm talking about palazzo pants: those flowy, wide-leg creations that became the rage in the early '90s (and have enjoyed several comebacks since).

I had climbed the ranks at The Gap from trainee to assistant, passing all of the requisite tests of sample closet cleaning, and running the OTB (open-to-buy, an inventory management tool). I had aced my stint as associate merchandiser of Socks and Belts (such a glorious title!) and was ready be prove my worth as a genuine "merchant" in the illustrious department of Women's Bottoms. I would finally get to select the next fashion trends for the store.

"The Gap is a denim company. We're all about natural fibers," my boss stated resolutely. "We don't like to sell anything that's not cotton. Besides, those things look like something you might wear to bed or see at Kmart."

I had first spotted these new elastic-waist printed rayon pants being worn by one of my hip neighbors in San Francisco. Unlike the brightly colored styles I had seen in the sleepwear section of department stores, these pants were a sober black-and-white print. What's more, she paired them with a fitted white T-shirt, giving the whole style a chic yet relaxed and casual air—*a perfect evolution for The Gap*, I thought.

My boss wasn't buying any of it until I asked my neighbor to lend me her pair so I could model them in the office. I found my coolest Tretorn sneakers and a perfectly white, cap-sleeve pocket T-shirt. I positioned my hands nonchalantly in the pockets and sauntered into my boss's office with the air of someone about to head off to the beach or on a stroll in a park. She looked up from her desk once, put her head back down, and then did a double take, as if seeing me for the first time.

"Wow! I never thought I'd like those but they're pretty cool. Wearing them with the sneakers and the tee makes a huge difference. I could totally see how it 'fits' in our Gap style. Let's call the New York office and see if our designers might want to create some summer styles."

The design was a huge success. We ended up selling hundreds of thousands of units and making a ton of profit (the simple construction ensured a low cost and the beautiful patterns allowed us to charge a lot). Most important, the introduction of this new trend helped to shift the perception of The Gap as a "unisex" jeans store to a valuable fashion resource for women. By seeing those pants as something other than pj's in the way they were worn, and resetting their context for my boss, I had picked the next fashion trend, influenced The Gap's business, and gained credibility as a legitimate merchant.

Once I grew beyond my role as a merchant, becoming a senior leader responsible for larger and more diverse teams, I often thought back on Roland Barthes's essay, "The Death of the Author." (All of those nights in the stacks of Sterling Library hadn't gone to waste.) Barthes claims the reader actually "kills" the author (metaphorically speaking!) as she weaves her own meaning from the words on the page. As radical (and scary) as this idea sounds, it served as a metaphor and emboldened me to broaden my definition of leadership when I found myself overseeing large teams with whom I couldn't interact on a daily basis. As leaders, we resemble the writers who certainly have some kind of meaning in mind—call it "vision," "mission," "strategy"—but our initial intent, no matter how perfectly crafted, is "put to death" as soon as someone else reads or tries to interpret it. And this type of "death" will inevitably happen, especially as your span of influence grows and your ability to monitor every detail decreases. As leaders, we *have* to have a purpose and a voice that we trust enough to put forth, just as any great writer or other artist might. But we must also realize that this intent never fully belongs to us alone; as it reaches our teams and the world at large, it is understood and reinterpreted in a variety of ways. So in a way, there is a "rebirth" of sorts inasmuch as your teams will invent and go forward with their own definitions of what you have created. Any good leader must own the "I"—who we are and what matters—but also "efface" or let go of the "I" so that others can appropriate whatever direction we're offering the company. Sounds good in concept.

Too bad I forgot this lesson when, as a first-time CEO, I tried to launch a leadership initiative at Chanel. The luxury business had been facing unprecedented and rapid change brought on by the Internet, globalization, and the economic boom in BRIC (Brazil, Russia, India, China) countries (particularly China). Everyone in the industry had been bemoaning the potential death of creativity in music, motion pictures, and magazines, and even on TV, as user-generated content threatened highly paid artists and higher-priced productions. Would anyone ever see our beautifully designed ads in the confusion and morass of information on the

Web? Would magazines forever shutter their presses and replace their glossy, stylized photos with Instagram posts and Snapchats? What about newspapers? Would information and opinions dissolve into a smattering of tweets and posts? Anyone could have an opinion about anything, any customer could log a complaint, any untutored "fashionista" could become an expert overnight, and any disgruntled employee could anonymously tell the world how mismanaged your company was. How could we ensure that our pristine reputation and image stayed intact? Meanwhile, an influx of new customers whose languages and cultures were less familiar now flooded our boutiques, challenging us to maintain our standards for attentive service. Increased demand, buoyed by Internet shopping, stoked the already vibrant market for counterfeit luxury goods; these days, if you wanted your logoed bag without paying the price, you could buy a fake, a lookalike, or just rent one from the comfort of your own home. How would we manage to maintain control, let alone grow our business, amid all of this chaos?

Everyone recognized the need to evolve and change the way we operated, and I had what I thought was an excellent plan. I would introduce a progressive leadership program that would integrate and support important values needed to encounter such disruption: attunement to keep pace with the fast-moving evolution in the markets, self-awareness to remain centered in our own brand's purpose, deep listening to hear opinions and understand desires of our newest clients, empathy to better understand the next generation of customers and employees, curiosity to explore innovative ideas required in this shifting environment, flexibility to move with such rapid change, and open-mindedness to consider multiple angles before making decisions.

On the surface, everyone agreed. But my initial approach led to one of the biggest face plants of my entire career.

First off, I chose a poor time and place—a foggy July day (the most stressful time of year, only a month before the standard French four-week vacation), in a cavernous hotel ballroom, its high ceilings punctuated with dusty, crystal chandeliers hanging like lonely ghosts of parties past. So much for setting the right tone. Without much input from the team, my coach and I had hired consultants, designed a program, and planned an intense schedule for the launch of our work. To kick the day off, we force-fed the team on icebreaker games in a rain-soaked garden. (Ever done any of those at your leadership retreats? If you have, you know how condescending and annoying they can be.) I then corralled the team into working groups to reflect on a series of leading questions with answers that conveniently supported my program. And then, to really kill the vibe, I took center stage to espouse my views on ways we would have to evolve to cope with this ever-changing, uncontrollable world. My team wasn't having any of it. The more resistant they became, the more defensive and emphatic I acted. I was so fiercely attached to my vision that I had apparently forgotten all I had learned from "The Death of the Author." I was now the one trying to control everything. What's more, I was *pushing* for leadership values that encouraged empathy, listening, agility, and curiosity while demonstrating the opposite. The ironies were hard to miss.

My instincts about our need for transformation might have been accurate. My arguments might have been solid. My material might have been meaningful. My intention was certainly good. But I hadn't embraced the very ideas my leadership program purported, nor did I represent the kind of leadership values I was asking my team to adopt themselves. As the day devolved into a stalemate and the energy drained from the room, it dawned on me that in order to lead such a major transformation, I would need to transform myself, too. I would need to search out and allow for the integration of new ideas and opinions, accepting that I didn't have all of the answers nor that I could possibly control the unexpected ways in which my message would be interpreted.

Days later, once home from Paris, I sat at my desk, staring out at the sun casting its golden glow over the trees. The scene calmed my senses, and still I felt the effects of my big mistake weighing on me. I'd have to start again. First, I fired the consultants and canceled my program. I would need to create something *with* my team, based on their feedback and the very particular context in which our brand operated. I still needed to convey the urgency of my vision—the need to evolve our leadership culture—but more important, I needed to invite and allow for others' points of view and interpretations. I crafted a letter to the team, reasserting my beliefs but acknowledging my missteps. I invited them to share their perspectives, and I enlisted each of them to help me design something useful. Together, we came up with a plan to launch a cultural change at Chanel that embodied our *shared* values and enabled us to tackle the very real strategic challenges we faced.

The process helped our team grow and reminded me that engaging in cultural change requires the participation of those who define it.

When leaders attempt to impose a strict point of view or plan, as I had done, their teams may quietly rebel, loudly disagree, or blindly follow orders. Either way the results can be disastrous. Command-and-control leadership, as it's called, doesn't allow others to think, create, or generate new ideas and eventually hinders the growth of the organization. Despite any orders, directions, or even suggestions you might give, you'll never fully comprehend how they come across or how others will implement them. And you certainly don't determine the outcome. Once *you* embrace this fact, you will find that the real source of your strength is to create the context in which others can insert their own meaning and invent even more innovative ideas or actions than the ones you may be envisioning. A little unruliness and plenty of open exchange don't just enhance the business, they also energize the team to become more resourceful and creative. Over the course of my career, I've resisted adopting what many experts call "leadership models" for this very reason. I have found no one right way to be, except simply *to* be and to express myself authentically—and to allow the same in others.

But this lesson doesn't just apply to leaders. Regardless of your field of study, your current job, or your career path, you can put this insight to work. How many times have you been in a situation where you explain a point of view and give all of the appropriate facts and reasons to support your argument, believing that you've been entirely clear—and yet your coworker or your partner completely misunderstands you?

Think about it. Suppose you have a great idea but a colleague just doesn't see it your way. You can fiercely argue your point, throw your hands in the air, and quit. Or perhaps you can invite your colleague to elaborate on her point of view to see if the two of you can create something even better. Getting stuck in a singular perspective, however right it might seem, is never as generative as inviting another opinion. Ultimately, you may still adopt your initial plan, but at the very least you will have tested the solidity of your argument.

When I get questions from students or young executives about how I got to where I am today, I can draw a line (albeit a little more free-form) from those many late nights spent in the library "stacks" to the person I've become today. Ardent proponents of STEM-based (science, technology, engineering, and math) education think that the study of the humanities is nice but not necessary, but I argue to the contrary. Every discipline in the humanities—literature, history, art history, philosophy, or religious studies—teaches us how to question how we see and interpret the world and who we are as human beings. These courses of study call upon us to become close observers of people and images, of circumstances, of the so-called facts, of variegated points of view. They ask us to draw relevant connections and to develop our own narratives about their significance. We do the same thing in nearly any business and in our lives all the time. Indeed, that's what all great leaders do, too—no matter whether they have a background in statistics or Shakespeare. Merchants and marketers need these kinds of skills to create the innovative products and images for their customers. And *anyone* working with other people—especially anyone hoping to lead others— relies heavily on being able to imagine what others may see, feel, and believe, even if they won't ever know for sure. If you are good at your job, you are always standing in the shoes of your customers, your team members, and your subordinates, your partners or suppliers, to see from their perspectives. You come to understand that your view is never the ultimate truth and that it shifts with the changing world around you. And if you are really good, like any accomplished author, director, or business person, you will realize that you are in a constant dialogue with, and relationship to, an audience and the world, co-creating through a set of infinitely changing ideas and influences.

How can you "be the camera," open your eyes wider to the world around you, and interpret the clues you might have otherwise missed? What "guilty pleasures" might you explore, which might seem, at first blush, irrelevant but could potentially influence your future? In what ways could you change the context of some aspect of your work or your life to give it new meaning? How might you see *yourself* in a different light?

◈

My college years at Yale reinforced my need to be near artistic expression and absorb beauty in everything I would do, but they also taught me a new, more subversive way of experiencing and understanding the world. "Subversion" is really about purposefully turning something on its head to see what will happen. To see things only in the context of how they've existed so far means limiting future possibilities. Though my nature is intrinsically rigged to push up against the conventional, I'd had little encouragement to explore that inherent bias, and certainly no philosophy by which to question it so rigorously. But as I explored the subversive nature of deconstructionism and began to apply its tenets to film and theater in terms of meaning making, I also began to see the subversive nature of any form of art, and the acute awareness of any artist of what has come before coupled with the desire to build on, react to, re-form, or transcend it.

I may not have known what I might subvert or transcend, but I was on my way to rethinking one particularly intriguing subject—what it meant to be a woman in a world so often defined by men.

THREE

Yielding to Chance

Fleur took a long drag on her cigarette. Holding the smoke in her lungs, she muttered, *"Est-ce que tu connais Paris?"*— "Do you know Paris?"

She spoke as if Paris were a close friend or a lover. When I sheepishly confessed that, up until a couple of weeks ago, I had only visited Paris for a few days before heading to the South of France but that I had been to the Louvre, the Musée Rodin, the Eiffel Tower, and the Arc de Triomphe, Fleur slowly released the smoke. She brought her hand up to her mouth and let out what sounded like something between a *tsk* and half a chuckle, her gesture conveying disbelief but also issuing a mischievous invitation. From that point on, Fleur decided it would be her duty to make my junior year abroad more than the usual jejune tour of moldy museums. She would introduce me fully and without any further restriction to what she called "PareebyNight."

For our first excursion, my new Paris roommate beckoned me toward her *mobylette,* or *mobe.* Unfortunately, this powerful step up from a bicycle didn't really have a back seat, but Fleur said that it wouldn't matter. If we were stopped by *les flics*—the cops—we would simply smile and convince them that we were on our way home. She had no problem using her feminine wiles to get what she needed. "I will also say that you are American," she said—as if that would help. Everything in life was like that for Fleur; it was about living the full experience, regardless of the risks or dangers involved. Not wanting to be a buzzkill, I hopped onto the back of her baby blue road warrior, the metal rack digging into my inner thighs. Fleur laughed, told me to get off, pedaled down the street to start the *mobe*, and then swung back around: "Hop on!" We sped off with a sudden start, as I grabbed on to her jacket and winced, thinking about the new bruises I was sure to have in the morning. But before I could worry too much, I put all of my focus instead on the whirring lights that passed as Fleur dodged in and out of cars. Lanes, stoplights, pedestrians—they didn't count as Fleur swung her *mobe* left and then right, taking possession of any otherwise un-occupied portion of open road.

We plunged into L'Etoile, the roundabout with eight lanes of traffic near the Arc de Triomphe. My eyes squeezed shut while I prayed we'd exit in one piece. Fleur explained the "rules"—I was not sure whether they were her own or written somewhere. No matter, Fleur felt most rules existed to be broken or at least twisted to one's advantage. As she explained it, yelling over the noise of honking horns and random cries of road rage, when en-tering L'Etoile, you needed to dodge as quickly as you could to the very center. "Never look left for oncoming cars," she yelled. "It's their responsibility to yield to you!" Once you've reached the center of the hub, she continued, accelerate as quickly as you can without allowing centrifugal force to tip you over. Aim for one of the "points of the star"—one of the many exits—turn in that direction, cutting swiftly and without too much concentration, through the oncoming cars, and then zip out of the circle. "You're actually supposed to yield to the right," Fleur explained, "but we will never get through if we do that!" No time for counting how many cars might careen into us at any moment. She just intuited her way through the oncoming traffic, with elegance, flow, and flair. I would soon learn how Fleur sailed through everything in life, despite any potential impediments, with equal parts of fierce will and innate agility. "And voilà!" You've arrived!

❖

I knew well before I attended college that I would spend a semester abroad—in Paris, of course. I would need, once again, to live in that beautiful and liberated culture I had discovered four years earlier. Our love affair was barely at the dating phase; we had just met, Paris and I. We needed to get to know each other. *PareebyNight, indeed.*

While most Yale students preferred English-speaking roommates, hanging out with other Americans was absolutely the last thing I wanted to do. I wanted to *be* French, not just study it. Much detective work turned up the name of a French student called Fleur—French for "flower," though I would soon come to understand the irony of that—whom I hoped to track down once I arrived in Paris and convince to take me in. Her name wasn't on the "approved roommate" list, but I managed to wrangle her mother's telephone number.

"*Allo?*" A giggly, high-pitched voice that sounded almost like a child answered the phone.

"*Bonjour, je m'appelle Maureen Popkin et je voudrais vivre avec vôtre fille,*" I said in my imperfect, nervous French. The conversation was particularly difficult because the word for "roommate" didn't even exist back then. (Now they say *co-loque*, short for *co-locataire*, or "co-renter"—you gotta love the French's absolute fixation on independence.). Besides not being able to translate "roommate," I had no other way to say what I wanted other than "I want to live with your daughter"—direct, to the point, if not a bit suspicious. Luckily, Mme Roux didn't take offense; she told me that I spoke French well and she would be happy to meet with me.

Mme Roux, an artist, lived in the 14th arrondissement about two blocks from her daughter. The late afternoon Paris sun laid a soft orange radiance over the paintings that covered the walls from floor to ceiling, and the ambient light complemented her red hair and the freckles that dotted her hands. Most of our time together, Mme Roux, her bright blue eyes sparkling, flitted around her apartment, gesturing to this painting or that while we discussed the virtues of impressionism. I worked hard to flatter her with my cursory knowledge of the movement (I had worked at the Saint Louis Art Museum one summer). Once in a while she brought her hand to her chin and fell silent, stopping to study a particular oil. After one such reverie, she suddenly jumped back into the present, remembering why we'd begun the conversation in the first place. She then dropped the bomb. *"Je suis enchantée de vous rencontrer mais finalement, l'oncle de Fleur va louer l'autre moîte de son appartement."* ("I'm enchanted to meet you, but Fleur's uncle has finally decided to rent the other half of her apartment.") I was crushed. Given the lively tone of our conversation and my interest in her art, I was sure I'd convinced Mme Roux of my worthiness to live with *"cocotte,"* an endearing, if not surprisingly sappy, nickname she used for her daughter. Fleur, I would learn, was anything but sugary sweet. Dejected, I trudged back onto the bustling streets, winding my way to the rue d'Alésia Metro and back to the hotel.

I was desperate to learn French even if I couldn't have a French roommate. As a last resort, I found an international Catholic girls' *foyer* (dormitory) in the 7th arrondissement where they insisted all of the students speak French. As I stood before the large wrought-iron gate in front of the simple, Bauhaus-like square stone building, I felt a twinge of disappointment; I'd imagined living in a quaint "old house in Paris, covered in vines" as I'd read in my beloved *Madeline* children's books. Instead I was greeted by a nun dressed in a neat habit who escorted me down an austere hallway toward my room, a barren white cube. On the way, a couple of students dutifully lifted their bowed heads with a *"Bonjour, ma soeur." Wait, would I have to call her "my sister"? Had I gone too far this time?* I worried I might be committing some kind of sacrilege against my Jewish faith, even though I was hardly religious. My suspicion was confirmed when we ran into an older nun, who was introduced to me as *vôtre mère* (my mother).

"I'm going to be living in a Catholic *foyer*," I told my parents when I called Saint Louis. "But honey," Mom said, "you're Jewish!" "Gee, thanks, I almost forgot," I murmured sarcastically under my breath, then added, "but they're very liberal here"—I hoped that was true—"and the important thing is that I'll learn French." (It's little wonder that I used the word "determined" to describe myself on a college essay.)

I struggled to greet the Mother Superior with "*Bonjour, ma mère*" and to understand the French accents of the other foreigners. It was on about the fifth day of my stay there that "*ma soeur*" told me I had received a phone call. Mme Roux's honeyed soprano voice came on the line. The uncle had decided not to rent half of the apartment after all, he was unreliable anyway, and would I still be interested? I felt like I would burst.

The first day I met her, I knew Fleur was different from any other woman I had yet encountered. After dragging my suitcases one by one up the six flights of stairs and unpacking my things in the empty bedroom of the small two-bedroom apartment, I heard the door slam. With a "*coucou*" (casual "hello" you usually use only when you know someone), Fleur peeked around the corner of my room and then, without invitation, came in and gave me a two-cheeked kiss hello. She insisted I come immediately to the kitchen, a tiny, narrow vestibule with the bare necessities of a fridge, oven, and stove so she could have a smoke and get to know me (read: interrogate me to see if I was cool enough to hang out with her). Fleur leaned back against the window, cigarette in hand, firing questions at me about food, parties, and school subjects. She held strong opinions about almost everything and made no excuses about anything she might say.

Fleur reminded me of the free and rebellious attitudes of the French women depicted in some of the New Wave films I'd studied. I remembered watching *Jules and Jim*, a film apparently about a love triangle, two men, best friends, sharing the same woman. But I found the title deceptive. Or maybe the title said just what it meant by omitting the most important character, Catherine. For me, the film was *about* Catherine, played by the captivating Jeanne Moreau. Or more precisely, the film was about the impossibility of defining Catherine, about the men who wanted to own her, about her incessant need to escape any distinct category.

In the beginning of the film, Jules describes all of his romantic conquests to Jim and finally, in frustration that he cannot find the right mate, sketches his ideal woman on a coffee table. Later, they both fall in love with a stone sculpture of a woman (fashioned by the hands of a man), determined to follow any woman who might resemble this unflawed vision of beauty. It seemed what these men most wanted was the *idea* of a woman, one who couldn't talk or even move but somehow conformed to their notion of perfection. No wonder their world was turned upside down upon meeting Catherine, whose brazen and independent spirit refused to be boxed in.

In one famous scene, Catherine plays a game with her two

companions. She disguises herself as a man, paints a mustache on her face, pulls her hair up in a newsboy cap, and changes into baggy pants and a button-down shirt. She strides onto the streets of Paris, where a man asks her for a light. When he says, *"Merci, Monsieur,"* she smirks at Jules and Jim, knowing she has won her little game. Who wouldn't want to be Catherine at that moment? She could inhabit whatever form she chose; she wasn't confined by classical representations of a woman. Beautiful, sexy, desired, loved, and admired—but out of reach. No box could contain her.

Fleur *was* a real-life version of Catherine, and in so many ways, my alter ego. She was blond, sassy, and a little wild but also blunt, pragmatic, and straightforward—unlike me, brunette, careful, calm, and an introverted dreamer. One evening when we spilled out of a late-night party and I had complained that the toilets were unusable, Fleur brushed it off with a flip of the hand, *"C'est pas grave. Il faut juste faire comme ça."* ("It's not a problem. You just have to do this.") The cigarette went into her mouth and in the same motion she unbuttoned her jeans, unceremoniously dropped her pants, and squatted on the pavement between two parked cars. When she was done, she noticed that I was wide-eyed with amazement. She just threw her head back and laughed. *"Et voilà, c'est une bonne chose de faite!"* ("And there, that's one good thing taken care of"), as if this kind of display were the most natural thing in the world. Other nights, I might find her lounging in the bathtub having a good chat with a guy friend sitting next to her on the closed toilet seat. I marveled at her complete nonchalance—in her mind, why wouldn't she use her time wisely? It didn't occur to her that I might not also take baths with my school friends watching. Or, adorned only in sheets, she would invite me to meet her new boyfriend after their lovemaking. All of these antics added up to more than just funny stories to tell my friends back home; Fleur was inadvertently teaching me about being comfortable and self-confident, particularly as it pertained to sexuality and the human body. She was never an exhibitionist but demonstrated a natural ease about who she was and how she expressed herself.

Fleur's attitude toward sexuality and her body changed the way I thought about being a woman. Up until this point, I had respected and followed the implicit rules for how I was "supposed" to behave. It wasn't that there were no role models back in Saint Louis. I did have one high school teacher, Ms. Moceri, a tiny, blond bombshell who always dressed in the very shortest skirts and most provocative, low-cut, colorful blouses. When she entered the room with her sultry gait and straight posture, her chin jutting slightly up, she exuded inner strength and a confident and powerful feminine energy. It was the first time I realized that as a woman, you could be completely feminine and yet completely in charge. Without raising her voice, she was nevertheless fierce and fearsome when grilling her students and grading the longer-than-average term papers she'd assigned. In my mind, she could stand tall next to any man without puffing out her chest or resorting to the usual tactics employed to establish "dominance."

At the same time, my Midwestern roots had taught me to be exceptionally careful about expressing my sexual desire (in fact,

I'd learned that I should suppress it altogether—only men were allowed to feel "that") and to be modest about my body. Even though my first experience in the South of France started to shift my ideas about nudity, I was still under the strong impression that women simply shouldn't display sexual desire in the way that men could. We could be seduced but not seduce. We could sleep with men if we loved them and were in a committed relationship; men could sleep with us for fun. Today perhaps we are more liberated to express our femininity and sexuality in less confining ways (although the myriad of reports about harassment and bias on college campuses and in the workplace indicate we still have a long way to go). But back then, before spending time with Fleur, I didn't even realize how ridiculously one-sided and prejudicial these principles were! These rules had been woven into the very fabric of my being, and, to a certain extent, I was incapable of deviating from them without a sense of guilt and self-reproach. Sexual harassment, as defined by law, is only a crime when it becomes a condition for employment, advancement, or education, or in one's living environment in such places as universities. But what conditioning occurs when such prejudices are so woven into our society and our everyday lives that we hardly notice them? We fail to recognize and consider how these quiet, unspoken societal norms infringe on our sense of self-confidence.

Fleur's élan was contagious. I started to imagine that I, too, could navigate the world around me in a less inhibited way and make choices without the burden of "have to," "should," and "must" that I had so readily adopted in the past. Fleur seemed to willfully ignore expectations and, in that way, she helped open my eyes to the possibility of finding something more authentic and real in myself. She rarely broke the rules for the sake of sheer rebellion. She simply refused to accept the barriers that prevented her from doing what she considered essential and even simply more practical. She had cultivated an intimacy with her wants and needs that allowed her to see the world beyond its obstacles, rigid structures, and set definitions. She ducked the turnstiles at the Metro station because she saw no reason to pay. She sunbathed topless at the beach not to make a scene but because she had no use for tan lines.

This combination of freedom and utility fascinated me and taught me to take myself a little less seriously (something I still need to keep in check). Until this time, I had lived with a strong bias toward working myself very hard and placing myself under the scrutiny of the highest expectations to ensure my success. Being in France, being around Fleur, showed me there were equally important lessons to be found in plunging in—to a new culture and new circumstances—without working so hard to do what was expected, what I thought was "appropriate" in order to move forward in life.

The ability to see beyond constraints, and to move through life in harmony with one's truest desires, matched with pragmatism, became a foundation for me, particularly in my orientation to business and my career. In the various jobs that I have had, I try to aim at what I hope to accomplish before finding reasons why it cannot be achieved. I've noticed that getting too caught up in all of the reasons why a particular desire cannot be fulfilled or a goal cannot be reached works as a self-fulfilling prophecy. It's a little bit like when you are skiing. If you begin to stare at all of the rocks, crevices, and obstacles, you're sure to hit one. If you focus on where you want to finish, your skis usually take you there without too much effort. Seeing Fleur glide through L'Etoile and so many other situations encouraged me to find my own sense of direction and my own way of navigating around the rules and labels that others might establish to block my progress.

My junior year abroad finally ended, after a glorious summer spent living like a true Parisian, never setting foot near another tourist attraction and picking up as much "argot" or French slang as possible. (To this day, I impress even the most jaded French when I resort to this street vocabulary, peppered with my best "Parigot" accent). I finally came to know "PareebyNight" by hanging out with Fleur and her friends, attending parties and letting loose in every and all variety of nightclubs. As to be expected, Fleur even managed to get us past the bouncer of ultra-exclusive, members-only clubs like the Chez Castel, a feat that afforded me the highest degree of cred. Sadly, it was time to return to college; once again I had to put my romance with Paris on hold. I might have to bend some rules to return on my own terms.

❖

As my senior year of college rolled around, I had no idea what I *could* do, given my intellectual interest in the dark and complex recesses of deconstructionist theory. Many of my friends seemed to have it all figured out well before the last semester of senior year. Investment banking and management consulting were the tried-and-true path, but neither seemed feasible for someone like me, who'd never taken an economics or math class. Still other friends had set their caps for some worthy profession like law or medicine and had aced the undergraduate requirements and standardized tests to go down one of those long and virtuous roads. Not me. I had no clue.

Really, all I knew was I wanted to go back to Paris. I *needed* to go back. I just didn't know how. So with no way to get there and very few options left before the end of the school year, I decided to do like so many others: take the LSAT and apply to law school. The notion of law school hovered over me like some misty cloud: present, visible, but nothing I could really grasp. My dad was a lawyer and an excellent one at that. A year before, I'd sat in the audience while he argued a case before the Supreme Court of the United States. It was one of Sandra Day O'Connor's first years serving as a justice and I remember watching her serious face as she took in my father's arguments and rendered what sounded like harsh remarks. After the trial, which my father won, he told me that she had ruled in his favor, "liked" him, and had said rather complimentary things. It didn't sound like that to me, but I trusted his way of hearing better than mine. You see, I wasn't entirely listening to the case; I was watching the dynamics of the judges, how they positioned themselves, what words they used, how the elegant sleeves of their black gowns fanned open when they lifted their arms. To me, the occasion was impressive, beautiful, moving—it was like theater. But could I see myself acting out scenes like this for the rest of my life?

I should have known better when, very uncharacteristically, I couldn't seem to make myself study for the big day of the LSAT. I didn't buy any of the available preparatory tomes to learn to take the test. I simply sent in my fee and showed up, as the French would say, *"y allant en reculant"*—"walking backward" into the entire process. The test was early in the morning, and I stood wearily in line to sign my name on a clipboard, feeling defeated before I had even begun. A disheveled fellow, probably a debt-laden first-year law student in need of extra cash, handed out the forms and issued instructions in a robotic, monotone voice.

The proctor gave us the signal, and with an air of resignation, I opened the booklet and jumped into the first question. I read the problem and then looked at the multiple choices below. None of the answers seemed appropriate or relevant to what I'd read. I reread the problem a second time, squinting hard as if to improve my focus. Finally, without much conviction, I selected one of the answers and moved on to the second question. After ten minutes, I'd barely answered three questions. The words on the test book-let started to blur. After about twenty minutes, now well into my sixth question, it became clear: I did not want to be a lawyer. I had no purpose here and needed to escape. Immediately. With the lightness of my new resolve, I rose, test in hand, my chair scraping behind me. A couple of students' heads popped up, then dropped back down over their tests. I noticed a slight panic come over the face of the proctor as he motioned me to sit back down in my seat. When he came over, I whispered in his ear that I was done and asked that they please erase from my records the results of my partially completed exam. The law student cocked his head a little to the side, lifted a tired eyebrow as if to say half-heartedly, "Okay, but you know you're making a mistake," and told me I could go. I strode confidently toward the door, ignoring any disapproving heads that turned my way.

Without any marketable skills—or so I believed—I went to the campus career resource center to see what kinds of jobs might be appropriate. The career counselor sat across a large desk and asked me a battery of questions that sounded like one of those "love match tests" you might find in *Seventeen* magazine. "So what do you like to do?" "Do you belong to any clubs?" "What are your extracurricular activities?" "Do you like to work alone?" "With others?" I answered all of the questions the best I could, hoping she could help me solve my dilemma. From the list of these thoughtful and probing questions, we homed in on a very important fact: I enjoyed "working with people." In the counselor's opinion, this "unique" quality opened up a host of "very interesting opportunities" that were located on the slanted metal shelves along the walls of the room. She encouraged me to look at the brochures from different companies that might want to employ someone who "liked working with people." I spent the next half hour thumbing through the dog-eared corporate material. I left more confused than before my visit.

I knew nonetheless that I wanted to make a mark, like the delicate impression my mom had done in plaster of Paris of my tiny foot when I was just an infant; I just wasn't sure what my medium might be. I briefly entertained the idea of working in PR—since I "liked working with people"—but just in the nick of time, Fleur saved the day by introducing me to her uncle, an executive at L'Oréal, who recommended me for an internship in—where else?—Paris.

❖

There is so much talk about "following your passion," but what if your passion doesn't immediately lead to a viable career or what if you don't know how to find the job that corresponds to something you feel deeply in your soul? I didn't have the answers right away but I knew where I belonged and was willing to risk nearly everything to get there. Sometimes, you have to take that first step without a fully formulated plan, follow your intuition, and be ready to go with the flow, just like plunging into oncoming traffic at L'Etoile.

It's odd. We usually imagine mentors as teachers, bosses, or other hierarchal superiors. We admire them, sometimes deify them, and often put them on a pedestal—believing they have all of the answers. But finding a mentor doesn't always mean approaching the highest-ranking, most successful person you know, nor does mentoring only occur when you happen to be sitting across a table in an office or conference room. Seeking out more unconventional, even subversive individuals who inspire and challenge you can provide you with plenty of street smarts for the moments in life when you need them the most. For me, mentors have come in all shapes and sizes and, as in the case with my friend Fleur, can instruct and inform you just by being exactly who they are and encouraging the same in you.

Today, I imagine that with a myriad of networking tools like LinkedIn and assessment resources like Glassdoor at your disposal, you may have managed to avoid the dreadful career services office as you plot your professional course. Maybe figuring out what you want to do is a little easier even if it is probably harder to actually *get* the position of your dreams. Or perhaps you've had an experience similar to mine, only behind a lonely computer screen at home or in some empty office. I have watched my own daughters as they struggle through nearly the same process of trying to figure out who they are, what they really care about, and how that becomes a job. Unless you've chosen to pursue a career where the milestones are perfectly clear—such as law, medicine, or academe—the path is inevitably difficult to navigate. Everyone has her own approach, but for me, it was first about getting crystal clear on what I *didn't* want, reaching a few layers down to understand what I truly desired (beyond the type of job itself—I wanted to be in France!), and then taking a giant step—albeit a risky one—toward what was calling to me. In the end, Fleur's simple advice may be the most honest and useful: when in doubt, *hop on!*

FOUR

Road Training

The next time I returned to France, it wasn't to catch a ride on the back of Fleur's *mobylette* but to take hold of the rickety steering wheel of a tin can rental car during my "stage route"—L'Oréal's six-to-twelve-month on-the-road training program for new employees. First-year marketing apprentices were deployed to the far reaches of France to sell shampoos, hair colorant, mousses, and skin creams to supermarkets and hypermarkets.

The marketing internship Fleur's uncle found for me was in the department of L'Oréal Parfumerie—at the time, the most important division in the company where teams of professionals conceived of worldwide, mass-distributed products and images bearing the L'Oréal name. Working in the marketing department of that prestigious division was seen as an important stepping-stone to running a bigger part of the business someday, particularly if you were a young man hailing from one of the top French business schools. Obviously, I wasn't a young man, nor had I gone to business school, but I was grateful to get a foot in the door of one of the best companies in France and eager, as always, to excel at whatever this new job would entail. While at first I chalked up my reentry to a stroke of good luck (there was certainly some of that), I realized that my persistence in finding Fleur in the first place and insistence on immersing myself in French culture (including those late-night parties) was about to pay off. According to some, having a *carte de visite* (a business card, literally translated as "visiting card," probably because they allowed access rights to most circles in Parisian society) from such an illustrious company opened doors all around France—if, that is, you made it through the various tests and challenges the training program threw in your path and learned how to play by their rules.

Nobody, no matter how exclusive their education, how elevated their academic degree, or how top-drawer their pedigree, could start directly in marketing without going through L'Oréal's rigorous protocol. Even prior experience didn't count. In fact, the higher up you were on the food chain, the longer your training period. L'Oréal wanted to be sure you were humble enough to see the value of understanding the business and its customers from the ground up. The company firmly believed that to market any of their products, you needed to see and experience where, how, and to whom these products were sold. As a consequence, they had designed a series of demanding hurdles all marketers had to clear. It was a bit like one of those video games where you must slay a certain number of dragons, run through a gnarly labyrinth, climb to higher levels of difficulty, and accumulate enough keys along the way to unlock the gate of the inner sanctum. On paper it all sounded great.

Until I understood what the first *level* meant: proving my worth as a sales rep in the Pas-de-Calais, North of France. Until this point, the closest *I* had ever come to selling anything, besides Girl Scout cookies during my short-lived career as a Brownie, was the summer I worked at Neiman Marcus in Saint Louis, spritzing oncoming customers with men's fragrances. Nose numbed each day by competing scents and feet weary from uncomfortable high heels, I had decided back then that a career in sales probably wasn't my destiny. Now, if I wanted to survive, let alone succeed at L'Oréal, it looked like I had no choice. I would be responsible for selling L'Oréal's finest wares to the hypermarket chain, Mammouth, in a part of the country where I knew no one and had never visited. I was intimated by the idea of driving through an unknown territory, selling beauty supplies out of a briefcase by day and sleeping in the French equivalent of Holiday Inns by night. And although my education in deconstructionism and New Wave cinema taught me about standing in another's shoes, at this point, the actual *standing* was purely theoretical. And yet here I was: cast out in the middle of nowhere, living out of my trunk, a postmodern version of Willy Loman in *Death of a Salesman*.

I was convinced that L'Oréal had deliberately sent me to a place where neither tourist attractions nor scenery could distract me from experiencing the *la vraie France* (the real France) and mastering the tasks at hand. Other trainees had been sent to Marseille, Cannes, and Nice—all sunny locations on the Côte d'Azur. Instead, I motored two hours from Paris across the sullen, cratered landscape of the Chti's (a rather obtuse word referring to the people and dialect of this region). Beside the stretches of girded concrete beaches commemorating the Allies' victory, this area bordering Belgium was best known for its low-ceilinged foggy days, row houses, coal mines, and high unemployment rate. No sun, no sea, no portside restaurants or late-night parties, just large expanses of flat land, grim brick homes leading to a center of town where a massive Gothic church or modest town hall might still stand. What's more, most of the hypermarkets were located far from these town centers on desolate, pitted farmland dotted with piles of coal debris from the long-abandoned mines. Map wedged in between my shaky legs, hand gripping the stick shift, I drove off each morning to visit my clients.

At first glance, the Mammouth outside Roubaix resembled many grocery stores I'd known in the United States, only it was a lot bigger. (True to its name, the word *Mammouth* translates to "wooly mammoth" in English.) The enormous parking lot spanned what seemed like miles. Coin-operated grocery carts revved near the entrance. Inside, endless rows of packaged goods, fruits, and vegetables had settled in every square foot of the building. The yogurt selection alone took up one entire aisle, every imaginable texture and flavor colorfully packaged and arrayed in columns. Odd smells wafted from the colossal cheese selection. But the real shock came as I made my way toward the meat section and spotted a skinned rabbit with black bulbous eyes glaring at me. Pushing past a selection of beef tails, wild boar, venison, pheasants, quails, and pigeons, I confronted a pig's head hanging on a metal hook from the ceiling, daring me to pass by without meeting his gaze.

Fortunately, my appointment was with neither the rabbit nor the pig, but with a very busy man named Mr. Dupont. He was the buyer for hair care products, sanitary concerns, and frozen peas. I had a fleeting fear that this eclectic buying responsibility might suggest my beauty products were not *his* first priority. I shivered from the cold air and jangled nerves, waiting for Mr. Dupont to emerge from the large metal double doors next to the kidneys, livers, and brains. Finally, he arrived in a smudged white smock and ushered me into a back room. I was ready, or so I thought. We were launching Studio Line, a full range of products from mousses to gels, and my boss told me that I needed to negotiate at least five *têtes de gondoles* ("heads of gondolas," a very romantic way of saying "end caps," the part of the aisle that juts out into open space and always displays the store's promotions and bargains) of this fluffy stuff in order for us to meet our monthly goals.

As I introduced myself, Mr. Dupont's face scrunched up as if he'd just tasted a lemon. *"Vous vous appelez comment?"* I repeated my name and he retorted, "What kind of name is that?" I wasn't sure how to answer that question. Did he mean my surname, the Russian Polish "Popkin," or the Irish name "Maureen"? He seemed slightly offended that my name wasn't easier to pronounce. He started to look over his shoulder as if an invisible boss might be beckoning him or the Green Giant rep had arrived, obviously anxious to get rid of me and to attend to whatever more important task I might have interrupted. *No literary criticism is going to get me out of this one*, I thought. This whole situation, far from the elaborate visions (well, illusions) I had in mind (my first real job in the City of Light!) was beginning to make me question why I had reignited my tryst with Paris in the first place.

"*Je suis Américaine,*" I finally told him. (I remembered Fleur telling me this admission would get us out of a potential bind.) He shook his head knowingly, smirked, then blurted out, "I love *Dallas.*" My mind froze in disbelief. *Dallas?* In the middle of Northern France, people were watching *Dallas*, the wildly popular nighttime soap opera? Okay, it was a start. Perhaps a little common ground. I took out my marketing pamphlet and told him how much volume, shape, and texture Studio Line Mousse might give his hair. While I recited these well-rehearsed lines, I could practically see my reflection in the slick black sheen on his head. *Probably a Brylcreem man,* I thought to myself. As he shifted his feet impatiently, I decided spontaneously to come up with a new argument, switching on the spot from articulating the many benefits of mousse to gel. He started batting his hand at what I thought might be a fly but then I realized he was shooing my "marketing speak." None of this marketing mumbo jumbo was going to fly here in the North of France. I was going to have to adapt to their way of doing things.

I put away my well-crafted arguments and simply asked him what he felt it would take to obtain an end cap during our promotional period. He hesitated, genuinely surprised that I was finally speaking his language, and threw out a percentage discount on his next order. We batted numbers back and forth, our fingers doing consecutive tap dances on our calculators until we found a number we agreed upon, then shook hands and parted ways. "*A*

la prochaine, L'Américaine" ("See you next time, the American").
And from that day forward, whenever I stepped inside that Mammouth, a sound rippled from the front of the store to the back—
"*L'Américaine est arrivée*" ("The American has arrived")—as the
team signaled my visit. Even the pig seemed to smile when I
returned.

When my boss heartily congratulated me, I felt relief and
pride at having passed this first test. I was mostly looking at this
road training as a necessary evil, merely as a springboard to
something better. Only later did I come to appreciate the value
of learning from the ground up. Seeing L'Oréal products in the
places where they were sold and getting to know the people
who bought them gave me insights into what kinds of marketing messages and packages we should develop to speak to our
customers' needs in their own language rather than resorting
to deadening marketing-speak. The carefully crafted marketing
brochures I'd been given might work in some instances, but not
on guys who sold frozen peas. I needed to learn *his* language to
meet my goals.

I found this approach equally powerful later in my career,
when I made it a priority to visit factories at The Gap or boutiques at Chanel. The people on the front lines, often ignored,
provide some of the most useful instruction into what's working
and what's not. It was also the likes of Mr. Dupont who taught
me that in order to sell anything—not just hair mousses or
gels—I would need to get comfortable with radically new and
sometimes adverse circumstances; I would need to remain open

and flexible when things didn't quite go my way, and to set aside my own agenda.

End caps confirmed at Mr. Dupont's store, it was now time to find a place to sleep. Because of the distance between this region and Paris, I would need to spend the entire week in the North before heading back to Paris on Friday evenings. Miles of empty road turned up only dingy, run-down operations hosting a few visitors a week. In a neighboring town I located an Ibis, an aseptic, simple chain of hotels resembling Super 8 motels where all of the other sales reps stayed, but I turned up my nose at the idea of sleeping in an American knock-off. I headed to Lille, the largest and most cosmopolitan city, where I was sure to find something more authentically French. Just as night was falling, I found an adorable little inn right in the center of town only footsteps away from the Grand Place du Vieux Lille, the large plaza in Old Lille. Despite the charming façade and inviting interior, the nightly rates skirted just underneath my per diem. *What luck*, I thought!

The front desk manager seemed happy to see me, asked about my accent, and was impressed with my mastery of French. She was even more impressed by my *employer*; mention of the company L'Oréal seemed to pleasantly surprise her. Pleased to find my cozy room furnished with delicate floral wallpaper, a small bed, fine cotton sheets, and even a genuine down pillow, I nestled in for the night.

Just as I was falling asleep, I was jolted awake by bangs and thumps and a high-pitched voice emanating from the next room. I put the pillow over my head, hoping the noise might soon subside. Unfortunately, the racket only got louder, the banging and thumping becoming more rhythmic, and the crying turning into a theatrical moan. A lovers' rendezvous, I supposed, on a late evening in Lille, maybe? Eventually, things quieted down and I fell asleep.

Delighted to have found such a quaint treasure, I decided to ignore the previous night's disruption. When I checked out the next morning, I did wonder what to make of the other hotel guests: women wrapped in cropped rabbit fur jackets, patent leather miniskirts, sharp *talons aiguilles* (stilettos), and fishnet tights, who flashed shy smiles my way before quickly throwing their keys at the front desk manager and scurrying off. I brushed away my suspicions, not wanting to be too judgmental. But after a few more noisy sojourns in this darling hotel, I finally asked one of the other sales reps in the area if he knew anything about the place. He looked at me a little quizzically and asked if I had stayed there. When I replied, "Yes, I love it," he laughed amusedly, *"C'est un hôtel de passe. C'est pour ça que tu entends ces bruits."* ("It's a bordello. That's why you hear those noises.") Abashed by my naïveté, I resigned myself to Ibis's white plastic palaces for the remainder of my field training. The French expression *"Il ne faut pas pêter plus haut de son cul"* ("You shouldn't fart above your arse") seemed especially relevant to me in this case.

In the end, the Ibis hotels weren't so bad; I became accustomed to and even appreciative of their cleanliness and regularity: one less thing to worry about as I made my way through the coal-mining towns between Mammouths. I even began to relax and look forward to what I might discover each day. One morning, as the sun was trying hard to break through a thick layer of insistent clouds, I rolled down the window to wipe off the accumulating condensation of the humid morning, breathing in the sharp aroma of this industrial swath of land. I tried to see the beauty around me, taking a page out of the book, or perhaps a frame from the reel, of my old friends, the New Wave directors. The shadows from tall utility lines draped over the uneven, paved roads, and, as the morning haze cleared, I noticed in the distance a neat line of low-lying foothills, the coal fields, darkened to a deep purple, as if the scene had been painted by one of the impressionists. I couldn't help but wonder, How *did* one define beauty? Does context determine beauty, or could it ever be the other way around? If I could see that range of mountains, those coal fields, for something other than what they were, practically speaking, could they be considered beautiful? It would be too easy to overlook what they *did* represent for many observers— hard labor, dangerous conditions, poverty, and pollution—but at the same time they evoked a peculiarly arresting kind of majesty in their own right. How often, in the rush of the day-to-day, do we pass by things offhandedly, labeling them "ugly" or "ungainly" without really looking at them or without considering other facets and definitions of beauty? As I got to know this area in northern France better, I thought wistfully back to the way those handheld cameras favored by New Wave directors revealed beauty in the grit, in the commonplace, in ways we might not have noticed before. Could we imagine that beauty itself doesn't just exist in society's version of aesthetic perfection? Beauty also emerges from places and things that tell us stories, that make us feel something or create a certain mood. Maybe the very fact that these purple majesties did represent such hardship made them beautiful because they stood for the narrative of those who lived and struggled there.

These past six months in the land of the Chti's had indeed been lonely and sometimes scary, but I had started to grasp its beauty, too, of a different and perhaps more profound nature. Like in those films I studied, "beauty" lay in the imperfections and the flaws that spoke to our lives and touched our hearts. I didn't have to be frolicking on a beach on the Côte d'Azur or visiting the spires of Lourdes to fill my senses or to learn what would be needed in my job. Not only did I gain practical knowledge for my next role, but I had also learned to reconsider and even to subvert my long-held ideas around the very definition of beauty. Imperfections and flaws, pitted landscapes and coal debris, could be seen as beautiful even if—perhaps *because*—their most prominent qualities stood in direct contrast to conventional labels and definitions. This realization would guide many of my future impulses as a marketer and a merchant.

Sales targets hit, I had proven myself and returned to Paris ready to apply my meager knowledge to the best of L'Oréal's products. Little matter that I didn't have a clue about what marketers did, besides create the pamphlets I used (or discarded) to sell my products. And never mind that I had never worked in the corporate headquarters of a big company. I had great hopes for what

I would find: a stunning office of my own overlooking the Eiffel Tower, a skilled assistant to help with the grunt work, and, of course, a seat at the table making big decisions.

Okay, I wasn't *that* delusional, although I did expect that in short order I would be able to put my experience to work. But for now the only thing I'd be applying would be hair colorants: sticky, gooey, purple, ammonia-smelling formulas.

In keeping with its philosophy to train marketers from the ground up, the next stage in L'Oréal's training program entailed two weeks learning how to apply the products one would eventually get to market. Widowed septuagenarians came to L'Oréal's private training salon to receive free color treatments. Clad in a spiffy white lab/beauty coat, I received them, offered a smock and shoulder protector "so we don't have any unfortunate accidents," and led them to a reclining chair, where we would chitchat about poodles, grandchildren, and politics as I squirted the purple stuff out of tubes onto scalps that were often unwashed and freckled with dandruff. My nose wrinkling from the strong ammonia smell, I would apply their preferred shade. Despite my amateurish efforts, the ladies were generally grateful. And ultimately, even if I might find less beauty in this particular task, learning to apply the products on real customers proved invaluable. Memorizing the ingredients in each formula and studying the directions for applying them would only get me so far. Actually getting my hands dirty (so to speak) gave me insight into how they would use formulas and what results they yielded—crucial information in developing any product, not just hair colorants. Still, at the end of the two weeks, I was ready to take off my gloves and leave the smock behind.

◈

L'Oréal's windowless corporate boardroom looked a little bit like a luxurious padded cell. The walls were paneled in soft Napa beige leather; fine stitching outlined each perfectly symmetrical square. A distinguished mahogany oval stretched the full length and width of the room; the lighting was deceptively soft, a gentle yellow that, if you weren't aware of what actually happened in this room, might convince you to make yourself comfortable. I had finally made it into the L'Oréal boardroom and was primed to make an important presentation—in the meeting they referred to as a Prospective Induction—to the CEO and regional directors.

As a newly minted assistant product manager, I felt the heads of all of the executive team members, all men, simultaneously turn on cue to look me over. From the tips of my brand-new black pumps to my newly acquired pink suit, their sticky stares followed me as I took my seat toward the front of the room. There I huddled with a few other new managers, waiting our turns. The meeting came to order when a young *chef de produit* (product manager) nervously stood up to present market research she had done to demonstrate the need for an important new product in an important segment of the hair care market: a shampoo that would appeal to the tween and young adult segment. Red splotches crept along her neck as she stuttered and sputtered her way through the data, the clicking of her tongue against the roof of her mouth discrediting her crisp slide presentation. The CEO abruptly cut in with a pointed question we all knew was impossible to answer: How would this product meet the needs of older women with colored hair? L'Oréal dominated the hair colorant market—my domain—and sales were on the rise in that category. The product manager's proposal for a younger market clearly held no interest at the time, for the CEO and subsequently for the eleven other men around the table who stared accusingly as she fumbled through a stack of hundreds of transparencies she'd brought as backup. After she spent a few prolonged yet fruitless minutes frenetically paging through her research, her boss stood up, silencing her with a look. No, he interjected, they hadn't looked at that segment of the market. A hush fell over the room. The CEO quietly called over the head of human resources, an older man with a roundish face and graying temples, who gave him a meaningful look from behind the thick frames of his rimless glasses. The day after the meeting we would discover the empty desk where this young woman used to sit.

No wonder my boss, William, had raked me over the coals for so many months about not knowing *my* facts and figures when we'd prepped for my presentation. I had thought he was just being unreasonably persnickety.

"I don't see any competitive research here," he'd snapped. He'd asked me to gather statistics on L'Oréal's competition, a request I had ignored because I couldn't see the utility of the data.

"We don't really have that many competitors," I had said a bit timidly. "I mean, Clairol is the closest one with only four percent market share in France." I wasn't entirely sure what terms like market share meant, but it sounded important, and it was one of the phrases more seasoned colleagues peppered their conversations with.

William sensed my discomfort and pushed harder. "You can't go into a Prospective Induction without a complete competitive analysis. You talk about share, but you're not showing year-over-year growth. And where are the full descriptions of their market position compared to ours? What about their customer segments? Their USP [unique selling point]? Their respective market growth?" He fired terms and lingo at me like tennis balls being spit out of a machine faster than I could hit them.

Somewhat cowed, I nevertheless continued to try to cover up my lack of knowledge, which only irritated him more. "Why look at competitors when we're so far out ahead? We have ninety percent market share," I said, using that term again to mask what I didn't know. "Does Clairol really mean anything in our market if barely anyone buys it?"

"You're not going to any meeting without a thorough and complete view of the competitive landscape; otherwise, it will be a train wreck," he scolded. "You can't assume that we will always be leaders in hair colorants. In order to build a brand, you have to know your customer, your market, *and* your competitors. Go down to the market research office and ask Caroline (my office mate) to help you." The machine was almost out of balls, which was a relief because I'd been swinging my racket in the empty air.

Now I understood that William's demands were coming from

the right place. He truly wanted me to succeed and was protecting me by insisting on what I needed to improve. His manner was more abrupt than I was accustomed to, but he was teaching me to think like a marketer and protecting me from self-sabotage borne of insecurity.

Soon it was our turn to present the new packaging proposal for Si Naturelle, a semipermanent hair colorant. I say "our" turn, because William and I had a slightly different strategy than the duo before us. He would go up to set the frame, give some background to our work, and remain at my side while I made my debut.

William didn't quite fit the L'Oréal mold. Instead of wearing his hair cleanly parted to the side, like so many of his peers, his was unruly, thick, and somewhat spiky. He normally pursed his lips, but when he smiled impishly, you noticed a slightly broken front tooth. His suits were not made of the same fine gabardine as the other group managers' but of a less structured cotton that showed signs of wear. The sleeves drooped softly at the shoulder and grazed the tops of his hands, giving him the look of a boy wearing a suit borrowed from his father. Unlike many of the other L'Oréaliens (yes, there was a word for those who perfectly fit the mold), William seemed proud to be outside the pack. Despite his differences, William was well liked by the CEO and other executives around the table, in part because he had gone to one of the two best business schools in France—Hautes Études Commerciales de Paris, or HEC Paris (as did almost all of the other people in marketing at that time)—and was smart and articulate. He had mastered all of the nuts and bolts of marketing but had something extra I hadn't noticed in the other managers. It wasn't just his confident smile and offbeat boyish spunk that seemed to amuse the CEO. William knew exactly how to toggle between conventional marketing vernacular and the less spoken language of aesthetics. He could recite any statistic or data point *and* talk about colors, fonts, and graphics in a way that the other group managers could not. Even more impressive was his ability to link some of these less theoretical and more intuitive arguments with just the right facts and figures to sell his proposals. It occurred to me then that if I wanted to excel at marketing and tap into my own creativity, I would have to strive to achieve this same fine balance.

I watched carefully as William began to build the story around our new product—a breakthrough hair colorant that allowed women six weeks of semipermanent color without damaging or drying out their hair. William praised the packaging for its "graphic tension," "nervous color," and other seductive terms. The CEO turned the packet over in his hand, screwed up one eye, and blurted out, "I think the red needs to have more blue in it and the font is too crowded."

I caught William's eye and allowed my shoulders to relax. The CEO was telling us that our product launch was basically a go. And the head of HR remained firmly in his seat, meaning that I could remain firmly in mine.

Eager as I was to take on more responsibility and to be given access to meeting rooms just like these, I now appreciated that it wouldn't be all fun and games. I had thought that getting into this room was the tough part, but being here, I realized that the game had just gotten more complicated and certainly riskier. This first experience was seared into my memory; the corporate boardroom was a place to be both revered and feared. Over the course of the next twenty years, I would make more than a few appearances in this room, each with their own quirks and atmospherics, but always with a mix of trepidation and ambivalence even as I eventually came to take a seat at the head of the table myself.

❖

Regardless of your position, your level of experience, your education, or your age, starting out in a new position is *never* easy. Awkward moments, blissful ignorance, bizarre rules and rituals, new lingo, explicit and implicit "tests," and subtle social cues—these are all par for the course. I wish I could tell you that once you're in the know, you're in the know forever. But that's simply not true. Later on when I joined The Gap and then Chanel, I would endure more trials and need to master other disciplines. No matter where you are and at what point you are in your professional development, this cycle of learning and unlearning is almost impossible to avoid. In fact, even if (or especially when) you've been in the same position at the same company, unlearning—challenging yourself to see issues in a new light—helps release you from conventional thinking and see opportunities you may have otherwise missed. It feels good to demonstrate one's mastery of a topic or a skill— that's part of the process training programs such as L'Oréal's help bring to pass. But the most successful people—meaning those who have long, varied, and fulfilling careers even if they never rise to the tippy top—embrace their own naïveté and use it to fuel their growth. In other words, they take the time to appreciate everyday observations—to see, for instance, that a coal-mining range might represent its own kind of hard-earned beauty. They reject the obvious in favor of the unusual, the extraordinary, the evocative, or the new. The artistic impulse begins with this attitude, and, as it turns out, so does the kind of creative thinking and innovation companies need now more than ever.

I was lucky that William appreciated my willingness to learn the ropes, to put in the time doing unglamorous work, and that he gave me the opportunity to test my skills and to figure out how I could begin to make a contribution to our product's success.

Now promoted to a product manager, I stood once again in William's office, prepping for another Prospective Induction. As before, he grilled me and pointed out logical gaps in my presentation. Our rehearsal was interrupted when our product's new packaging prototypes arrived from several of the creative agencies we'd commissioned. Usually, William viewed new mock-ups alone in his office, savoring the moment to develop his point of view before anyone else distracted him. More than once I had found myself hovering around his doorjamb, in hopes he might invite me in. This time his excitement outweighed his patience and desire for privacy.

One by one, William took each pack out of the tissue, picking carefully at the tape holding the wax paper in place, as if it were some delicate wrapping paper he wanted to save. He held each pack between the very tips of two fingers so as not to touch the fragile stenciled type, then lined the packs along the edge of his desk. He separated them in groups by creative agency, like different battalions of soldiers, each bearing unique color uniforms and varying stripes. A few moments after eyeing the troops, he pulled forward a couple of the fortunate and handsome infantrymen—the best packs from each agency—separated for further inspection. I sensed that I wasn't allowed to say anything because that might interrupt his thought process. Instead, I moved to stand slightly behind him, peeking furtively at the packs, my own eyes squinting as if mimicking his gesture, so thrilled was I to be privy to these important decisions and to see how a *real* marketer went about it.

"Do not tell *anyone* you have seen these," he said. "They are very preliminary. What do you think?"

I was shocked that he wanted to hear my opinion, but I was eager to share it. "I really like that tone of red," I blurted out without thinking too much. "It feels warm and vibrant. The cursive font is cool and young, but it seems too crowded."

William paused for a minute and looked up at me, as if seeing me anew. He seemed pleasantly surprised at my response. "Hmmm. True, but I also think the diagonal is too steep and gives a sharp appearance to the photo that it's framing. I think we should ask them to rework it."

He said "we"! I thought. Did this mean that I was his partner now in this work? I could feel my spirits lift to the sky.

"Next time the design firm comes," William said, "why don't you sit in with me so you can see how they work."

FIVE

Finding Your Groove

I could hardly see where I was going as we slithered our way like sidewinders through the crowd to an open spot near the front of the stage. Wisps of smoke from glowing white cigarettes wound their way toward the blue lights in the ceiling. James ordered two gin and tonics while the waitress wiped down the sticky table with a dank cloth. I tried to make small talk, but James's eyes were on the drum set onstage.

We were at the Blue Note, New York City's most famous jazz club, to see Dizzy Gillespie's show after a long day in the studio. I had worked side by side with my boss William for the last two years, and now here I was in New York, representing L'Oréal at the photo shoot that would launch the marketing campaign for our newest product, Si Naturelle.

We had elected to shoot in New York, home of all of the hot models at the time, and by some miracle I was allowed to go in William's place. I would be working alongside James, our advertising agency's creative director. To save money and be close to the studio, we had reserved rooms at the storied Gramercy Park Hotel, which boasted an elegant, star-studded, albeit slightly ill-reputed history. The property had fallen into disrepair after its glory days in the fifties but remained a bastion of decadent cool, even if the carpets were stained and threadbare and the guest rooms reeked of stale tobacco and cheap whiskey.

No matter to me: I was thrilled to be so close to the action— exploring the creativity that brought magic to our products; how, in the language of some of my more business-oriented colleagues, a value proposition became a marketing campaign. Who better to show me the ropes than James? Preparing for this shoot had brought us together as close colleagues and friends.

James was tall, around six foot two, but his shoulders tilted forward. I often wondered whether his pose conveyed resignation or casual cool. Was he on the verge of collapse or so self-assured that he didn't need to act the part? His oversize tortoiseshell-rimmed glasses accentuated his protuberant blue eyes. As he entered a room, he seemed to be pitched to one side, one of his long arms dangling at his side, the other one hefting a large black portfolio case. The cuffs of his striped Brooks Brothers shirt were frayed at the edges. His gray flannel pants hung neatly but loosely on his wiry frame. He always wore a thin leather tie, his trademark, which stood out against his otherwise button-down appearance. Everything about James fascinated me, but I was particularly drawn to his incongruities; he was both distant and present, permeable and resolute, neat and messy, visionary and pragmatic.

One thing absolutely unequivocal was James's passion for jazz. When he wasn't teaching me how to evaluate fashion models, print layouts, or photography, he was educating me on his favorite musicians, from Charlie "Bird" Parker to Art Blakey, from Miles Davis to Dizzy Gillespie. After a long workday, we'd often end up next to his record player, drinking wine and talking over the blare of trumpets, the squeals of saxophones, and the hiss of snare drums. James would select the next album, pulling it from the sleeve as if it were made of the most fragile glass, and placing it carefully on his professional turntable. He used a felt brush to clean each of the records, pointing out how even a tiny particle of dust could affect a one-of-a-kind groove. "Each record has an individual sound, almost like a DNA," he explained, "so if you buy a new one, it won't be the same as the one you already own." He'd gently lift the needle, and, with a steady hand, lower it into place on the track he wanted me to hear.

James didn't just listen; he let the music envelop him. He told me stories about these famed musicians, occasionally stopping mid-sentence to say, "Okay, now, here it comes"—and he would beat the air with his invisible drumsticks, hit the invisible cymbal, pump his foot on an imaginary pedal of the bass drum, and pause, arms in the air, to slow the beat with his illusory snares. Sometimes he ceased talking altogether and drifted off into a jazz reverie. He admired the musicians' technical prowess, but it was the emotional impact of their rhythms and melodies that moved him.

And now Dizzy was standing just a few feet before us. My mouth stung from the first sip of gin, and I felt my cheeks flush. *Cheeks.* Dizzy's ballooning cheeks had become his trademark, producing a sound like no other trumpet player's. His renditions were exciting because they kept you guessing; he would race along gaily, blaring boisterous staccato notes with piercing clarity, and then slow the pace down to a moody lament. Indeed, that's how he got his nickname—meaning, he often left his audience dizzy with the exhilarating turn of events his performances produced. When he first walked out on stage, his jowls hung loose, deflated. He ambled from one side of the stage to the other, razzing his band and cracking jokes. And then he started playing. Eyes shut, Dizzy's sagging cheeks became reanimated as the room swelled with "Night in Tunisia."

I had heard "Night in Tunisia" in several recordings but something struck me this time that I hadn't noticed before. Even as the melody remained recognizable, different players ventured into a series of unrehearsed solos, spontaneously coaxing the melody into surprising new directions each time. The other musicians followed along, adjusting their own playing to enhance the soloist's improvisations. As the riffs got wilder, it was hard to anticipate just how the players would bring the main melody back into tune, but they did, and then they'd be off again, headlong into some thrilling new groove. I asked James how it worked. He explained how the musicians had mastered their instruments, the music, and the techniques required to play with absolute perfection. But the real magic, he insisted, came when they improvised and landed on unorthodox connections that took the players, and the audience, on a ride to new territory. The basic structure provided by the score is important, he maintained, but it's just the starting point. The beauty of the experience comes when they start pushing up against those musical forms and conventions to create a sound that might seem a bit unruly at first but then becomes something truly mesmerizing.

In this way, jazz was like my beloved French New Wave films. At heart, both forms derived their emotional resonance from subverting convention. First Godard mastered cinematography; then he disrupted those techniques, giving the audience an emotional charge that shocked, surprised, and often delighted them. And now here were Dizzy and his band using subversion to deliver their own unique emotional charge to the audience. Both were inviting us to look and listen in entirely new ways.

Isn't that what all great artists do? Isn't that, to some extent, what great marketing does, too? It catches our attention. It throws us off kilter. It shakes things up. A great marketer has to learn the rules, to read the score, as it were, before trying to come up with her own riff. But coming up with an original riff is, ultimately, the whole point. Ask customers what they want, and they'll tell you pretty much what you expect to hear (i.e., something matching the attributes they desire). But ask them what they crave, and they may not know the answer. Great marketers provide products and communication that have unexpected, and therefore compelling, emotional appeal.

Indeed, if you only memorize the score, you can be sure to hit the right notes, but will anyone remember your bland tune? The creative spark depends on patience, persistence, and practice, but you have to be willing to take risks, too. To improvise requires having a sense for where you want to go, then letting that resonance emanate from deep within yourself, the place where love for *your* sole expression resides.

◈

In my two years learning the right notes as a marketer, I still couldn't bring myself to emulate the other *chefs de produits*, who always seemed to be singing from a different songbook. I respected their extraordinary expertise, their wielding of pie charts and acronyms, but I wanted to find some way to express my fascination with creativity and still assert myself as a marketing professional.

I wasn't an artist, but since I adored being around them and had such appreciation for their talents, I began to develop personal relationships with the designers at the creative studios, acting as an ally when they needed support or guidance. We talked about their inspirations in art, pop culture, fashion, or music and their creative struggles as they tried to work within the constraints of our design specifications. My primary responsibility was to nail down details and ensure we met deadlines, but I didn't want to follow the lead of many colleagues who, like generals in the army, barked orders, battled over deadlines, and worked to bend the will of the designers to their own preconceived (and often uninspired) notions of what was needed. I started to discover how to subvert the rules and create the context in which the design team could invent something inspirational. I learned that asking them what they most believed in, highlighting what was beautiful in their designs, and asking them to amplify *those components* yielded more positive and exciting results. But it wasn't quite a free-for-all: I still had to help them strike the right balance between exploring new territory and hitting our requirements. This would prove to be good practice for when I became a leader at The Gap and Chanel and would have to cultivate creativity, lead diverse teams, and make the numbers work all at the same time. I would have to give my team room to experiment and grow, but gently guide them when goals weren't met or they strayed too far from our original purpose.

Too much of the time, however, company leaders get nervous about unorthodox or unconventional pursuits; risk-averse and often uncertain about their own vision (and their own careers), they inadvertently squeeze every drop of creativity out of innovative endeavors. I have seen the negative effects of this dynamic countless times in my career, but the first was at one of L'Oréal's advertising meetings where the top brass confronted the outside agency. That's where I first encountered James.

These meetings usually began with firm, serious handshakes, pleasantries proffered through tight smiles, and nervous chatter. As people settled into their assigned chairs, James paid no notice, preoccupied as he was with making perfectly aligned piles of his mock-ups, which had been mounted on black boards for presentation purposes. In this instance, the campaign was to relaunch one of L'Oréal's best-selling brands. Peter, a short man and the head of the agency, looked like a cross between a bulldog and a marshmallow. He gave a verbose and emphatic introduction to the project, highlighting the agency's "deep understanding" of our number-one position in the hair colorant business, their "absolute, unwavering commitment" to L'Oréal's hair colorant products, and their "unflinching desire" to honor our request to create a campaign that would both protect and modernize the brand. Eventually, he handed things over to the forgettable account manager, who marched us all through a forgettable reframing of the brief we had given. Everyone except James sat with their arms crossed in front of their chests, impatient to see the mock-ups he caressed.

In one fluid motion, James rose from his chair, briefly tapping the pile before him nervously. Sensing that the room was not automatically on his side, his chin tucked in, his long fingertips tenting the edges of the table, he began: "This campaign is about bringing out the beauty in every woman. It is not a question of age but one of luminosity and brilliance. We tried to illustrate this through photos showing how beautiful hair brings to light a beautiful woman."

James lifted the first black board off the pile, revealing it as if it were a precious painting he was presenting to discerning collectors about to bid.

Arms remained crossed. Silence.

He began to explain the agency's approach. "We feel that showing her at a slightly profiled angle, not directly facing the camera, speaks to how the coloration unveils her beauty."

Still nothing.

He tried again. "This color of brown hair reflects the light so beautifully and brings forth the richness of shades from reds to oranges."

Crickets.

"Jessica Sorrenti is a young American model who is just start-ing out, but we felt she had just the right combination of sophis-tication and youth for this campaign." You could hear a pin drop.

"She has so much presence and just comes to life on the page." A slight shakiness rattled just underneath the surface of his soft voice.

The assembled twitched and fidgeted, waiting for the *directeur général* (general manager) to render a verdict. After a lengthy pause, he spoke, cocking his head and pointing his sharp index finger at the picture. "She has a funny hook in her nose and the big gap right there makes her hair look too thin."

Peter, whose presence had dominated the meeting's opening moments, was now a chameleon, his gray suit blending right into the wall as if he had ceased to exist. The account manager looked from side to side, as if pondering whether to make a run for the door. All eyes were on James.

The critiques came pouring in now, each with more biting lan-guage and cruel disapproval. Once the GM had finished, it was the marketing director's turn. "This picture is so completely dif-ferent from our brief. Why isn't she smiling more? We explicitly said that we wanted a girl who was expressing joy and enthusi-asm." He flipped open the folder where he conveniently produced six copies of the original marketing brief to prove his point. "If there are no better photos than this one, we may have to reshoot the campaign. And this will be the agency's responsibility."

James's shoulders drooped as he bent his head back to the

pile of black mounting boards, singling out one of the boards at the bottom of the stack. "We did a couple of other shots with Veronique, just in case." He then went to the next pile of photos and revealed one of a blond woman whose broad, toothy smile beamed directly at the camera. No one could deny—it was a very pretty photo of a very pretty girl with very pretty hair.

More silence and finally, "Well, that's a bit closer," the GM announced, as he studied the picture. "At least she looks happier and I think the blond hair makes her seem friendlier."

Nodding commenced around the table.

"Yes, this is definitely closer," the marketing director quickly agreed. "Can we see the other pictures of her?"

"Of course." James acquiesced and pulled out three or four pictures of the blond woman whose windblown hair looked as if each strand were held up by invisible strings. The marketing team seemed pleased with the pictures and congratulated the agency for work well done. "I completely agree," said Peter, suddenly distinguishable from the wall like some superhero who shed his invisibility shield. The group now all congratulated themselves on such a promising success.

And yet I could see that James was only partially satisfied. No doubt he was relieved to have pleased the client, but I knew he didn't think their choice was the best one. Their preference was a safe and logical bet, but it was the wrong one. It was Jessica Sorrenti's "aliveness" that drew your eye. It was the fact that she wasn't too perfect that made her perfect for this campaign. I saw what James meant by her presence. I felt his integrity at that moment and a sincere desire to support him in articulating it.

Watching James in that meeting, appreciating the purity of his intent, the wholeness of his own purpose, made me want to know him better and to learn how to gently encourage and guide him rather than take him down. Not knowing exactly how I might get to work with him, I began simply by positioning myself differently in the agency meetings. I wanted the creative team to know that I was on their side, and not just figuratively. Whenever James made a presentation, I would catch his eye to tell him without words that I agreed and liked the same things he did. If the occasion permitted, I would point out something beautiful about the images he was showing (a skill I learned with the design agencies)—something no one else saw but that I knew he might appreciate. Instead of obsessing over details and particulars, I tried to focus on how the picture made me *feel*. I tried to speak as a woman who might actually be making a purchase, imagining how I might like to feel when I chose the product. These may seem like small gestures, and they were, but it was my way of encouraging and supporting James so that he had the freedom to show us what he truly believed in and not just settle for the far less interesting work on the bottom of the stack.

William had noticed that I was developing a good rapport with James and asked me to work directly with him on selecting the fashion models for our photo shoot. He now considered Si Naturelle my product and my responsibility, a mark of his confidence in me. I met with James regularly to go over his "books"—

professional pictures and headshots—of our prospects. I had no idea what to look for but yearned to see through his eyes, so at first I sat quietly while he turned the pages slowly and methodically, studying each one, his fingers like delicate branches cradling the book as he considered contrasting visions all at once.

James embraced a sense of paradox in his work; he had his own aesthetic view but also listened to the needs of the business and integrated them into his reflections. Sometimes James would gently correct my opinions, grazing with the tips of his fingers the areas that might be problematic in a shoot.

"I don't think they will like her chin. It sticks out a little so it may be distracting."

"They may think her hair is too thin and since they want the fan on it, it will be hard to make it appear thicker without major touch-ups."

"Since the brief is asking for young, happy women, I worry she looks too serious. But see this girl?" He pointed to a model with a large gap in her teeth whose eyes sparkled with joy. "Now, she's beautiful. Her face lights up the picture." When I replied, "But what about the big gap in her teeth?" he chuckled. "That's one of the things that makes her so exceptional."

At first, I was uncomfortable talking about the "girls" this way. When I mentioned my concerns to James, he paused and gazed at me, something he did often, as if my words took their own time floating toward him. Then he laughed and said, "Really? *Mais c'est pas méchant*" (literally translated to "But it's not mean," but more figuratively something along the lines of, "I'm not trying to hurt anyone"). "This is their job. They are paid well. You have to think about their faces and bodies as their tools to create an aspiration."

Tools to create an aspiration. This phrase gave me pause. I had always thought of models being used for their beauty, but James turned this notion on its head. *They* used their beauty to create something for others—a stronger and more empowering view of women. This notion writ large—what marketing was *for*—would end up shaping my perspective as I continued my journey in the world of fashion.

Moreover, working with James made me question what distinctive tools I might use in my job—whether I could bridge the gap between creative and marketing and whether this might not be my unique contribution to business. Was it my job to reinforce the status quo or to figure out a way to be truly different—to put forth the exceptional part of myself for the benefit of others? As James's look books showed, there was plenty of talent and smarts in the world to match the standard brief, but that wasn't enough if you wanted to make your mark in the world, to offer an original vision or a new voice.

James was going for something beyond logic. He wanted to elicit feelings, to create a story that resonated with the viewer through a series of images. When he reflected on the qualities of different models, he spoke of what they "gave" the camera and how their features would contribute to the feeling he wanted to evoke, not whether their features were "pretty" or "ugly." He explained how one girl might work better because her smile brought her whole face to life or how another girl's vibrant allure came through her eyes. James never forgot that he needed to balance his artistic view with a more rational, market-driven one, but he didn't let that stop him from focusing on story and emotion, to reposition flaws and mistakes as trademarks of originality, beauty, and strength. These were some of the incongruities, the acts of subversion, that had come to distinguish him as an exceptional art director.

As business people we are all well versed in the language of logic and reason because we must explain our strategies, justify our choices, and gain approval of management, and yet we are surprised when we become locked into one way of seeing things. We tend to be preoccupied with checking off boxes from the design brief; indeed, we've already painted a picture of what we think the customers will want, and we can't help but be disappointed and to take objection to the work when it finally comes to fruition. Ironically, the best results never resemble the brief. In fact, as I've told many of my colleagues over the years, you should be very careful what you wish for: it might come true, but it will almost always be infinitely less interesting than when you let the creative team have free rein.

This overly constricting marketing frame, when skewed too heavily toward the analytical and rational, loses the equally valuable emotional quotient. Good marketing allows us to focus on a message or a point of view by emphasizing the clear differentiating factors of our products and by creating an entire ecosystem of images, packaging, and narrative that vivify the emotional charge you're trying to create, no matter how ephemeral.

Nothing is fixed. Our notions of what is beautiful, intriguing, or captivating are constantly changing. So, too, are our notions of what the "rules" are and how they might be subverted. What shocked art patrons in the 1800s (impressionism) seemed staid in the mid-1900s when the cubists gained attention. Had someone shown a Picasso to a man living in the beginning of the nineteenth century, he certainly wouldn't have called it "beautiful." But it was shockingly new; it sparked a new conversation, leaving its mark on future generations and, not so surprisingly, it created a new set of rules that would need to be broken by someone else down the road.

Subverting convention isn't just relevant in the arts. It's critical for consumer businesses, too, where choice is driven more by desire and aspiration than by logic and fact. Letting go of fixed expectations, or at least being willing to suspend them for a time, allows the possibility for an act of creation to surprise us, to leave us dizzy with the excitement of discovering something new that, somehow, feels just right, as if we were waiting for it all along.

❖

The morning of the photo shoot, James and I took the freight elevator up to the top floor of an industrial warehouse a few blocks from our hotel. As we exited the elevator, "Some Girls" by the Rolling Stones hit us in the face. The studio space occupied a vast open area that had been left in its raw state. Most of the windows had been painted over in black and everything else but the gray poured-concrete floors had been painted white, even the exposed piping overhead. We weren't alone. Several guys in low-rise jeans, white T-shirts, thick black belts, and assorted chains and carabiners dangling from their belt loops hustled around, carrying lighting equipment and adjusting the legs of various sized tripods set up around the stage. Two workers perched on ladders attaching a large section of white paper to a metal frame with a giant clip, while a couple of others checked the lighting with handheld monitors as they circled the space. An enormous black metal fan stood whirring in the corner, blasting each passerby with a mighty wind. Everyone seemed exceptionally busy and rushed, even though it was only eight a.m.

Young girls dressed in Flash Dance leggings, baggy sweat pants, and rumpled T-shirts, their hair loosely tied up in messy buns or pigtails, formed loose knots around us—all of them otherworldly tall and thin, but otherwise unremarkable, except for their surprisingly splotchy skin. (I later learned that this was normal due to the oily nature of the foundation used in photo shoots and that we could "get rid of it later" by "touching up" the photos.) I couldn't imagine how these young girls would be transformed into the glamorous women meant to decorate our packaging until we went into the small room where a couple of the girls were getting ready. One girl was "getting hair" and had giant rollers on her head. Nodding in the direction of a man wielding a canister of hair spray, James whispered that Alessandro was one of the top hairdressers in France. "He can work miracles," James confided. The gold canister seemed to be welded to his left hand, his own magic wand that could make thin hair look thick and almost any style seem natural despite using a full can of this stuff a day. I could already taste the sticky aerosol spray in the back of my throat.

We loitered around for what seemed like hours until Dan, the photographer, was ready to show James the lighting. The production assistant (the only other woman working on the set, besides the models) posed barefooted on the white paper while a light technician took a reading and Dan snapped a Polaroid and gave it to James. I wondered what it must be like for this nondescript thirtysomething wearing a shapeless cardigan to be around all of these beautiful young girls. No one noticed her face, only the reaction of light in the photo. I consoled myself by remembering how James described the girls' beauty as tools to create an image, not as some kind of definitive judgment or assessment of their personal worth. James gently blew on the Polaroid until it was dry, then brought it near the light box. He called Dan over to suggest he tone down the green; "you know how sensitive they are to green undertones."

When we were ready to shoot the first girl, the music was turned up about fifty decibels, and the production assistant brought the first girl into the white space. I hardly recognized the disheveled teenager from the elevator. Even her gait changed from giraffe to gazelle. Her skin was as pure as fine china; her jet-black eyelashes long enough to swat flies. Her lips, plump and apple red, glistened in the bright lights. I hoped that the result would not be vulgar—I never liked so much makeup—but James reassured me that what we see in real life is not what the camera picks up.

I watched as the model moved to and fro, swung her head, put her hands in her hair, and pivoted her shoulders, all the time flashing a big-toothed smile toward the camera. How exhausting, I thought, to have to hold that smile for so long, especially when the gale-force wind of the fan probably made her eyes sting. After several poses, one of the technicians scurried off and returned with a table for the model to use as a prop for some shots. The rest of the day proceeded in a similar manner with each girl in several poses: fan on, fan off, table in, table out, hair brushed, hair looser, pivot, jump, lean, sit.

I was surprised by how technical a shoot actually was and how hard everyone worked to make it possible. Seeing the process in every detail gave me a clearer understanding of what it takes to produce such beautiful images, but I could never imagine being so involved in all of the minutiae of putting together a campaign. What *I* truly enjoyed and where *my own* talent lay, I was now discovering, was in deciding *where* we wanted to go, identifying what kind of expression we needed to have, selecting the best choices, and then cultivating the end result. I was less skilled in determining *how* we might get there, but my ability to adapt an artist's perspective turned out to be just the rule-bending talent that made me stand out. My capacity to straddle both worlds and perspectives—marketing and creative, rational and emotional— was already starting to shape the way I worked and my professional choices. Over time, this ability to think like an artist without having to be one myself—to speak more than one language of business—would become one of my trademarks as a marketer, but even more so later as a merchant when I would need to follow the instructions of Mickey Drexler, CEO of The Gap: "Buy it like you love it." Numbers and analytics might be important, but how you felt about a product drove your investments and usually led to the most breakthrough results.

So, what's your trademark? How can you bend the rules to create something more compelling? What traits and talents might you be able to use to define success on your own terms? What "music" enters your soul and tickles your heart, yearning to be called forward and put to use in your job? What part of yourself can you bring to your job that creates your singular identity? And through whose eyes can you look to stretch your ability to see and find these things? What passions make you dizzy with excitement and expectation? Let's hear you riff on those.

SIX

A Fine Line

L unchtime has always been a very important moment of the day in France, and even more so at L'Oréal, where *la cantine* was no mess hall but a high-end cafeteria serving only hot meals with choices like *poulet rôti* (roasted chicken), *onglet de boeuf à l'échalote* (hanger steak with shallots), or *saumon à l'oseille* (salmon in sorrel sauce), all accompanied with a choice of creamy mashed potatoes or crispy fresh-cut *pommes frites* (an entirely different species from the French fries you find at McDonald's). No one followed the vulgar American tradition of eating a sandwich or salad at their desk. A full three-course meal was de rigueur, always taken in the company of friends and colleagues, and seasoned with gossip and talk of weekend plans. There was no talk of work itself, but plenty of conversation about who was dating whom, what executive might be eyeing which young new trainee as a possible new target for seduction, and where and when the next party would happen.

"Le poulet, s'il vous plaît," I told the server. Roasted chicken in France had a different flavor and texture than the broiled fare my mom used to make. I thought it might be the lightest option

until the server scooped a generous portion of mashed potatoes on my plate and poured the thick drippings over the entire dish. "I'll just skip dessert," I thought, turning away from *mousse au chocolat*, slices of *clafoutis* and lemon tart, three kinds of yogurt, and *fromage blanc* with raspberry coulis. Almost everyone drank wine with lunch. And if you didn't, particularly if you were asked out on a business lunch (*déjeuner à l'extérieur*, literally translated as "lunch on the outside"), you were considered rude. Despite my all-things-French immersion program, I still couldn't go that far. I grabbed a bottle of Perrier and followed my friends as we made our way through the maze of tables in the crowded dining room, dodging an occasional hand gesticulating with the crisp end of baguette. I concentrated on balancing my tray to avoid some of the more brazen ogling. As a young woman in a company focused on beauty, run mostly by older male executives, you could hardly avoid their scrutiny.

Then I saw *him*.

It was as if the clanking silverware and noisy chatter suddenly stopped. Actually, it was as if the entire cafeteria became still. He looked up at me. I returned his gaze. We only locked eyes for a moment, but his regard felt different from the flirtatious stares and desirous glances I and other women had grown accustomed to receiving during the course of the workday. He seemed to be looking beyond the obvious, inviting a deeper connection than I'd had with any guy up to this point in my life. It was as if he wanted to know me and see *me*, not just appraise the legs underneath my pink skirt. Little did I know then that this man Antoine would become my husband and partner in a new life.

I wasn't new to the dating scene in Paris while working at L'Oréal. Continuing to tag along with Fleur to various parties, dinners, and clubs, I had dated a fair number of eligible young men with what might appear to be perfectly suitable qualifications. A noble name starting with "de" to indicate his family used to own land. A vacation house on the Normandy coast near Deauville, a preferred spot for Parisian high society. Clean swept, side-parted hair, brightly colored pocket scarves, Weston loafers, and a hint of Hermès cologne. Smart, cultivated, and well-mannered, they weren't bad guys (most of them), but they all fit the same mold. I never felt that any one of them cared to know much more about me than what lay beneath my silk blouse.

Although his appearance was neat enough, Antoine wasn't a true "L'Oréalian." He had broad shoulders but a slim waist; his suit jacket fit snugly on top and roomy through the middle. The first button of his collared shirt gaped open to accommodate his strong neck and slightly rounded shoulders (he played water polo for years on the French national team). He leaned forward with both elbows on the table, an etiquette no-no in France. I would soon learn that he, like me, abhorred these kinds of rules. His plate was piled with *fromage blanc*, a cross between yogurt and cottage cheese, into which he had been dipping (God forbid) his half-eaten banana, now suspended in the air while he chuckled about something with his friends.

Antoine's professional trajectory had veered away from conventional choices. He had just returned from his two-year *Coopé* (a shortened word for *Coopération*) in Thailand. *Coopération* was a way to do requisite military service in France by working in the private sector. These posts were in high demand, both cushier and more exotic than the grueling physical training of regular military service; and because there were few spots available, many young men landed these positions through family connections. Not Antoine. He disliked what he felt was an unfair system and took pride in securing his *coopé* as well as his employment at L'Oréal without any help from family or friends. He loved Thailand, he told me, finding the lifestyle free and liberated, the people open and kind. The carved cupolas of the wats (temples) on the river, the sight of humble monks dressed in orange, the humid air, the bamboo homes, the whir of overhead fans, the colors and smells of fresh tropical fruits sold in the floating market, and even the seedier sights of Patpong, all spoke to something deep inside of him. Even now, two years into this stint at L'Oréal, he dreamed of returning to Thailand. That's why he'd requested to work in L'Oréal's export division rather than the more coveted "global" area (the so-called royal path, which garnered more attention by the higher-ups) in favor of travel and exploration. But each time he returned to Paris, he felt suffocated by the overly strict, sometimes unspoken rules and more rigid, closed-minded mentality of many of his marketing colleagues. He had asked his boss to be expatriated to any Asian country whenever the opportunity presented itself.

I decided that our first encounter must have been a fluke or just wishful thinking on my part because months went by before I saw

Antoine again. Then one evening, he decided to tag along with our mutual friend, Ravi, who had agreed to give Fleur and me some tips for an upcoming holiday to India. When Antoine spent most of the evening flirting—not just with me but also at times with Fleur—I was convinced that I had misread that first gaze; perhaps he was like all of the other guys I had met. But later that night, once we had all disbanded, he called me to apologize—in English to be sure only I could understand when Fleur and I both picked up the phone. He pleaded to see me again. When I refused, he persisted, calling me every day for the next several weeks, sometimes just to say hello and often to promise I was his only real love interest. Finally, after about three weeks, he called with a different purpose. His voice was hoarse and sullen.

"She's passed away," he whispered into the phone. Despite my rebuffs, I had started to look forward to and enjoy our brief telephone conversations. But his tone was different now. "I need to see you. I haven't told anyone else. I don't know why but I want to tell you about her. It's my aunt, my godmother. One of the most important people of my life. She was a strong woman, like you. Please agree to see me. It would mean everything to me." There was something about the tenderness in his voice, the trust he demonstrated in telling me, and the vulnerability he offered that melted my resolve.

I agreed to meet him just once, and just as friends, at La Closerie des Lilas, a famous brasserie, home of all of the great writers, artists, and intellectuals, on the edge of the 5th arrondissement. We sat at Ernest Hemingway's table, etched with names of former patrons and marked by a small gold plaque bearing the writer's name. As Antoine recounted tales of his childhood and affectionate and profound moments in conversation with his aunt, I was drawn to him the same way I had been the first time our eyes locked. He leaned over to kiss me and, this time, I let him.

Over the next year and a half, we fell in love and started living together, albeit surreptitiously. L'Oréal shunned intracompany relationships despite the overt flirtations and visible seductions over which no one seemed to bat an eye.

One evening, Antoine came home from work, his face white and the blood drained from his lips. I feared some awful tragedy.

"*Je suis pas bien*" ("I don't feel well"), he said through glassy eyes. I immediately put my hand to his head, relieved that he might just be sick. No fever.

"What? What happened?" My heart pounded as I braced for the worst.

"They offered me a job. It's a promotion." He fell silent again and looked away.

"*Mais, c'est genial!*" ("But that's great"). I tilted my head, searching his eyes to try to understand.

"It's in Jakarta," he said, glancing quickly over at me, his head bent down as if ashamed by the news. "It's for marketing director of Indonesia."

I felt like my heart had stopped beating. I didn't know what to say. He took my hand. I could tell he couldn't speak. We were both on the verge of tears.

"I mean, that's great," I muttered again, barely forming the words. "It's . . . it's what you've been asking for," I stuttered, not thinking it was great at all, but not knowing what the right answer might be.

"What are we going to do?" he finally said softly. "I love you and don't want to leave you."

"I love you, too, but I can't go to Jakarta. What would I do there?" I knew absolutely nothing about Indonesia and couldn't see myself stopping work to join him. He was getting the opportunity of a lifetime in the place he loved most. I wanted to pursue a career and knew it wouldn't happen if I moved there.

"I don't know. I need to think. I need time." He squeezed my hand and wrapped his arms around me, holding me tight.

Without knowing where my words came from or what they meant, I said, "Listen, I'm in love with you. I know you're the only one for me, but I can't try to sway you one way or the other or we may both regret it. You have to do what's right for you. If you think it's a great opportunity and it's what you want . . ." The rest of the sentence got stuck in the back of my throat. "But I can't go to Indonesia. I just don't think it would be a good idea." In reality, I wanted to scream at him not to go, but I just knew I couldn't ask him to pass up this job.

A week later—after much deliberation, fretting, and consulting his family—Antoine told L'Oréal he wasn't taking the job. He would have to leave the company since he didn't want to compromise his integrity, having initially requested and now having been granted expatriation. He felt his future was with me and as much as he was still intrigued by Asia, he wanted us to build a life together. He also understood that I wanted and needed to work. Already he was seeing us as equal partners, cocreating our relationship, instead of assuming I might jump off the career train to follow him, as so many women at the time readily did. I had never felt love like that from any guy I had dated. It went beyond love; it was the purest form of respect. I sensed even then that we shared a rare bond, one that would allow us each to pursue our ambitions and support each other in achieving them in whatever shape they might take.

Now I had a choice of my own to make. Antoine asked that, in turn, I leave L'Oréal so that we could move away from France, start a life together, and immerse ourselves in a new culture. In so many ways, it was a choice between the two great loves of my life so far. I was deeply in love with Antoine and certainly tempted by the idea of a new adventure, but I was still infatuated with Paris. My job was going well enough; I was receiving excellent training, and I still had a lot to learn and room to grow. For the first time, I had to think longer-term about my future, because despite all that was going well, I did have some concerns about my own career trajectory. As I looked around, I saw plenty of professional women working at my level, but they never seemed to make it much farther up the career ladder, at least not as frequently or as rapidly as their male counterparts did. Obviously, matters are quite different at L'Oréal today; the company is considered best-in-class in sponsoring women executives through multiple internal and external efforts. But in the mid-1980s, the chances for advancement beyond a certain level seemed pretty slim. I hadn't planned on leaving right away when Antoine's promotion came up, but several other incidents persuaded me that it was time for something else.

The first was during the launch of Si Naturelle. I was poised to present the new product with all of its marketing collateral to two hundred sales reps (predominately men). It was my very first speech in a large public forum, and in French to boot, so naturally, I was frozen with fear. I had been reluctant to use a teleprompter because I thought reading from a screen would detract from the immediacy of the discourse, but the tech guy reassured me that the focus wouldn't be on my speech anyway, his voice thick with a seductive undertone. Because this type of comment was common, I brushed it off, hoping instead to prove him wrong by captivating the crowd with my presentation, not my looks. The day of the launch, I stood at the podium, waiting for the text of my speech to appear on the screen before me. Taking three deep breaths to calm my nerves, I began reciting the words as they scrolled on the teleprompter.

Two sentences in, the screen went blank. There had been a technical glitch. I stood alone onstage, wordlessly, dry-mouthed, with a cold sweat trickling down my back. Just as I was about to retrieve the pages of the speech I'd stashed under a chair backstage, the tech guy bolted onto the stage to rescue me except that his attempts just made matters infinitely worse. As he and another techie knelt near my knees at the podium to locate the electrical problem, snickers and jeers rippled through the crowd of sales reps. From their vantage point, it looked like the techies weren't after an electrical issue at all but rather gazing up my skirt. Humiliated and now more resolute than ever, I grabbed the pages of my speech, booted the men offstage, and did my best to read the pages. Compliments abounded when I finished, but I couldn't help noticing that most of the audience continued to whisper and laugh as I struggled to read. Obviously, the little snafu onstage was infinitely more entertaining than my thoroughly prepared launch pitch. No one seemed to care about a word I said.

I asked many female colleagues how they handled all of the obvious attention paid to their looks, not their work. Some enjoyed the praise, taking it at face value, while others, like my office mate Caroline, were offended but thought it best to ignore it and get on with business. That's just what she urged me to do when, out of the blue, I was invited to an important executive lunch with a certain Monsieur X, a powerful man in the top ranks of the company. I had received a most beautiful envelope in the mail. My fingertips tickled as I ran my hand along the expensively textured stationary. Exquisitely handcrafted calligraphy spelled out my name on the front and the folded card inside employed a formal French, one used for grand occasions like weddings or baptisms.

At first I was proud to have been chosen to attend this luncheon, but then I felt confused. Why would he request my company? I asked Caroline what the invitation meant. She flapped her lips with a resigned, hissing noise, as if letting air out of a tire—a gesture the French use when circumstances defy easy solutions. It's their version of "whatever."

She tipped her cigarette into the ashtray and revealed a sly grin. "Ah, *ma chérie*, you *are* a bit naïve. Why do *you* think you are invited? *De toute façon, c'est comme ça. Il ne va pas te mordre.*" ("Anyhow, that's just the way it is. He won't bite you.") Her sarcasm stung me, but her resignation to the circumstances hurt me even more.

I doubt she saw it that way, but her indifference epitomized a tone I'd started to notice in many of my dealings with colleagues and executives, men and women alike. Being perceived as little more than "arm candy" or becoming the butt of a lewd joke was harmless and nothing to get upset about, at least as long as it didn't cross some invisible line into full-on harassment. That's how the reasoning went. But where exactly is that line? When your looks draw more attention than your hard work, what kind of signal are you being sent about what really matters? It's one thing to be respectfully appreciated for your appearance or for your femininity, but when these are the only terms on which you're judged, the effect can be stifling, even debilitating. I was grateful for the positive feedback I had received for my work, and perhaps Monsieur X's intentions were innocent, but I just couldn't bring myself to passively accept that this was the ways things were, or had to be, as I continued to pursue my career. I thought back to the conversation I'd had with James when we evaluated prospective models for our photo shoot: I felt like I was *being used* for my beauty, but unable *to use* my "beauty"—my real assets (intelligence, character, judgment, and taste)—to make a contribution.

For me, and I suspect for many women, such treatment produces a doubly damaging effect: I felt like I would have to work harder than most men to be recognized for my achievements and earn a place at the table. And, I had to be on guard about my physical attractiveness, lest it detract from my professional credibility. I had to walk a very fine line, one that so many women still find themselves having to walk to this day: remain open and friendly, acknowledging and maybe accepting the flirtatious attention (so as not to be seen as too belligerent or uppity), but demonstrate an unfailingly serious and sharp focus. Not so simple.

The truly detrimental effects of this perilous balancing act really hit me even harder at another professional event, held at the famous Hôtel de Paris, a palace and casino in Monte Carlo. I was congratulating one of my colleagues for the superb presentation he had just delivered. After a pause, his hand brushed my shoulder lightly, *"Tu viens avec moi au casino ce soir?"* ("You coming with me to the casino tonight?") Perhaps it was just a French way of saying it, but I noticed in the question an implicit assumption, the *"est-ce que"* being eliminated, as if it were not really a question but something I was meant to do. Still, I gently excused myself.

So he leaned in closer, now bringing his hand down over mine and giving me a little tug. Before I knew what was happening, he'd begun to guide me through the crowds. I kept trying to convince myself that we were just friends and that he just wanted to show me the immense gambling rooms, the women in long gowns, the men in tails, and the sparkling chandeliers. But once we entered the casino, he put his hand on the small of my back and eventually slipped it around my waist until his body was pressing into mine. I felt his breath on my neck as he pulled my hair back to kiss me.

I stopped cold. "You know I have a boyfriend. I'm not going to kiss you. I knew I shouldn't have come."

"Ah come on," he crooned. "You are so beautiful. I've always wanted to ask you out."

"It just isn't right. We're here for work and I have a boyfriend."

"It's just one night. No one will know. I know you are attracted to me. There is clearly something between us; I've noticed." He continued to stay uncomfortably close.

I pulled away, told him that it was time for me to go to bed, and that I had no interest in pursuing any romantic relationship with him. He finally conceded and gave me the standard French two-sided kiss, only he brought his hand to my face, cupped my cheek, and said, "*Tu es trop mignonne.*" ("You are too cute.") Shockingly, my rejection had only partially dissuaded him. He continued: "Well, if you change your mind, I'm in 701. I would really love to spend the night with you. It could be incredible."

I broke away and went to my room, relieved to find myself alone in the quiet, cool space. As I was getting undressed and ready for bed, the phone rang.

"Have you reconsidered yet?" the voice on the other end said. I had no idea how he found my room number. I began to feel ill at ease once again.

"No, really, I'm going to bed now. See you tomorrow." And I hung up.

At first, I tried to follow the advice of my office mate Caroline. I would simply ignore the incident, figuring it was just part of working at the company. *It happened all the time.* Besides, I told myself, my colleague was not trying to hurt or offend me, and he hadn't attempted to stymie my career or retaliate after that evening, and . . . after all . . . I had accompanied him to the casino of my own free will. I had pushed him away, that's true, but I was still a little flattered by his attention. No big deal, right?

Sitting alone in my hotel room that night, something started to gnaw at me. I didn't acquiesce to his overtures, but somehow it felt like I was the one who had done something wrong. I began to worry that I might have misled him. Was my dress too sexy, were my heels too high, my makeup too alluring? At that point I realized that I was buying into the very system that disgusted me. The problem wasn't that he tried to seduce me but rather that he assumed I would so obviously want the same thing. Because these acts of seduction were seen as normal and fair game, I began to see my own femininity as shameful, even dangerous, something I should hide or obscure. It made me feel less, not more, powerful, because it brought unwanted attention that, in turn, detracted from my competence and my self-esteem.

Antoine had shown me an alternative. He appreciated my looks *and* my brains; he saw me as a whole person, weaknesses and strengths in tandem. He accepted who I was, all of me, and supported the contribution I wanted to make. His willingness to consider my career as important as his encouraged me to hope for and expect something different, not just in my romantic relationship but in my working environment.

The prospect of leaving the city of my dreams and my job was still hard to fathom and many at the company thought it irrational, even possibly reckless, to quit so soon from my plum position. L'Oréal was a blue-chip company; I had a prime spot in the best division, in a domain that I actually loved. In my three years there, I had received exceptional training in marketing, and I had learned from the best of the industry about how to create the highest-quality products, combined with exquisite art to entice women around the world. I had grasped the importance of listening and responding to a consumer, not just through analytics and market research but through an intuitive sense, an ability to put myself in her shoes, to invent something that might speak to her heart. The experience had given me practical tools, but it had also illuminated who I was and what was vital to me. Yes, I needed to be close to creativity, I needed to work in a place that valued beauty, but I also needed to be valued for who I was and for my ability to do important work—a lesson I would return to many other times in my career. Choosing to leave with Antoine wasn't so hard after all.

❖

Challenging circumstances and discomfort are often excellent teachers inasmuch as they require us to get closest to what we fundamentally care about. In fact, if it hasn't already happened at some point, you are likely to face a time when you feel less than fully valued, not respected for enough of who you are or for the contributions you might make. These clarifying moments can be scary, which means you have to pay even closer attention to them and not resort to explaining them away or hiding from your own discomfort. Sometimes, they'll tell you it's time to move on. In other instances, they will guide you to stick it out, stake your claim, and create value in the job you have.

These types of decisions become infinitely more difficult later in life, when they affect not just you but possibly your employees or your family. Maybe it's not another person seducing you, but another job, a new company, in a different location or domain that beckons. Or perhaps, you'll be flattered by attention paid for the wrong reasons. You'll have to decide what means the most to you. Learning to reflect on *your* core values early in your career helps build the muscle you'll need later when the trade-offs are more significant and the solutions less obvious.

At twenty-five and without a family to support, this particular choice was relatively simple, but as I moved farther along in my career, the consequences and ramifications of this type of decision point became more critical, particularly when I was making another choice—what life might look like after The Gap. I learned that the most important thing wasn't the decision I was making but my ability to reflect on what was driving that decision.

Working papers being our only limitation, Antoine and I took our small savings and booked a flight to the United States, where we got married and bought a car. Our heart lines pointed us toward San Francisco.

◈

We arrived in July, before the season of fog; the crisp blue sky and colorful row houses glowed with the promise of new adventures. Only things weren't going to be *that* easy. With only a few months of savings, we couldn't afford anything but a bed and eventually a camping table, which we used alternatively to eat frozen pizza, iron shirts, and refine our résumés. Neither of us had bothered to research what kinds of companies were based in San Francisco before we moved, and now we realized there were slim pickings in the packaged goods arena. Convinced that I had found my calling as a marketer, I interviewed at Clorox, even if I wasn't terribly enthusiastic about photo shoots of mops and toilet bowls. It didn't matter. They didn't hire me because, without an MBA or American-style training, I didn't fit their criteria.

I was just beginning to wonder if we had made a huge mistake when, walking down Market Street, I spotted a black-and-white poster that stopped me in my tracks: Miles Davis, head in his hands, a sad soulful look in his eyes, in a black T-shirt. The image was signed "Gap" and one of many, all artistically shot in black and white, of noted individuals expressing their styles and personalities. Besides making pocket T-shirts cool, the campaign conveyed that The Gap was a place that honored individuality and brought out the best in people. Maybe I could "market" The Gap!

After landing an interview with the head of HR, I learned that

Gap didn't have marketing, only advertising, and that "I would make a perfect 'merchant.'" I had sworn off working as a salesperson after that summer working the perfume counter, and the word "merchant" sounded awfully close to being a salesperson. Still, those beautiful posters and the more attractive clothes I'd seen when preparing for my interview stuck with me. Within a week, I was back for my first interview with Millard (Mickey) Drexler, the CEO.

I am not sure what I expected when I first walked into his office, but it certainly wasn't what I saw. No pin-striped suit or neatly printed tie. Dressed in faded jeans and a perfectly pressed, untucked button-down white shirt, Mickey swiveled back and forth on his chair as he took a phone call, one hand lightly grasping the telephone cord while the other flipped through a catalog. He wore a neatly trimmed beard, which made him look more like a hip grad student than a CEO (not that I had had much experience with CEOs at that point). Occasionally, he let out an animated, "No way! You're kidding!" as his eyes got brighter. I stood in the doorway, not wanting to disturb him, even though his conversation didn't seem too serious. No grandiloquence, just down-to-earth real language. I wasn't used to hearing higher-ups speak with such simplicity and lightheartedness. He waved me in, as if we had known each other all along.

Mickey stayed on the phone for a few minutes while I admired all of the beautiful objects in his office. A faded antique globe, an intricate model sailboat, and black-and-white framed photography. Before the phone was set back in the cradle, he stood up and extended a friendly hand. "Hi, I'm Mickey." And so began one of the best interviews I have ever had.

His questions left me breathless. "Where do you like to shop?" "Why do you want to work here?" "What do you think we should change?" "What would you do if we hired you?" "What are your favorite brands?" "Who looks good out there?" I could scarcely formulate my responses before the next question, like a delicious jelly bean, was lobbed my way. His pace was impressive, but I was even more impressed by how much he cared about my opinion.

"Did you like living in Paris? Did you ever eat at that bistro Chez Georges? Best French fries ever, hands down." Wow, he actually wanted to get to know me.

"Paris was great." I tried to keep up with pithy one-liners so I could hold his interest but wasn't sure what might come next. "I went the first time when I was sixteen and knew I would always go back." I stopped myself mid-idea. He was still waiting for my answer on the food question, which seemed to interest him more. "No, I don't know that one. I like this little place on the left bank called Le Sergent Recruteur because—"

"Oh, I know that place. Isn't that where they bring you baskets of sausages and stuff? It's on Île Saint-Louis right near that great ice cream place where everyone waits in line . . . what's that place called?" He snapped his fingers loudly. I would grow to appreciate the various permutations of those snapping fingers in my years as a merchant. With Mickey, it was generally a sign that he loved what you were showing or saying. He seemed engaged.

"So, why do you want to work here?"

I had to think fast and make my explanations succinct enough for the fast-talking Mickey. "I left for Paris three years ago and Gap was selling cheap-looking clothes, tons of brands and records. I came back and now the clothes look cool. It feels like something new is happening. And the ad campaign is really great." Boy, I felt dumb. *Cool? Great?* I wish I had more time to come up with a better answer.

Snap, finger point. I guess he liked my answer anyway. "Follow me," he commanded.

Before I could ask where, Mickey was already telling Stephanie, his assistant, that he would be in the BR (whatever that was) conference room if anyone called. She should let the DMM (another unfamiliar series of letters) know he was going to look at the new bag collections. Mickey moved through the brightly lit, open floor plan, lifting his hand to say something to each cubicle occupant. "Hey, how ya' doin'?" "What's happenin'?" "Johnny-boy, what's up, man?" He knew absolutely everyone's name and occasionally paused for an answer. He didn't expect drawn-out answers, but I learned that day that the classic "nothin'" was unacceptable—because for Mickey there was always something new to learn. He was forever hungry and curious to get the vibe on what might be working or not working. And everyone's opinion counted.

"What d'ya mean, nothin'?" he said to one of the cubicle dwellers. "Somethin' has to be happenin'." The nervous fellow looked over the top of his beige cubicle partition at Mickey and immediately spouted out something like, "We sold forty-five thousand pocket tees yesterday. Teal blue is 4.0 weeks on hand." I had no idea what this unfamiliar language meant. Mickey bit his lower lip, gave a thumbs-up, but then caught himself and said, "You didn't buy enough. When can you get more?" By the time the answer was available, we were well down the hall.

In the elevator, his hands jammed into his pockets, resting his foot against the back wall, Mickey said, "We're going to see some new bags for Banana Republic. Just tell me what you think of them." He bounded out of the elevator as I tried to keep up, jogging awkwardly behind in my black pumps and suit. Almost everyone else wore jeans and stylish tops, though some of the women still wore skirts in neutral colors with simple details. And there were no high heels . . . anywhere.

Once Mickey pushed open the door of the conference room, the five or six people chatting and arranging the bags on the tables stopped abruptly and turned toward him with broad, nervous smiles.

"Hey, how's it goin'? Max, man, how'ya doin'?"

"Great, Mickey, did you see how the new safari jacket is doing? Blowing out, two weeks on hand." (I later learned that "blowing out" meant selling fast, and weeks on hand referred to inventory levels.) Fluent in this special language, Max answered Mickey like a pro.

Snap, point. "Cool, really? Go get it. Let me see it."

Max motioned to one of the other people in the room. "Go find the Kruger Park Jacket." The young man took off in a near sprint out the door.

Mickey turned to me. "Okay, Maureen, this is a test. Tell me which group of bags you like best. There's no right answer. Well, maybe there is, because I'm sure one looks better than the others. But you can tell me which one you like best. And don't worry if you think you'll offend these guys. They're cool. They can take the feedback."

There's no right answer? And I'm supposed to pick a product solely on how it looks, not market data? Now he was speaking a language I appreciated and could understand.

Max came forward and started to explain, "We call the first group the Rain Forest Expedition. The fabric is one hundred per-cent water repellent. The large duffle has a number of pockets." He began to unzip the bag to show me what was inside.

Mickey interrupted him mid-sentence. "Stop. Stop. Stop. No selling, Max. A customer isn't always going to have someone standing there to tell her what the bag does and doesn't do."

"Okay. I just wanted to show her the features," Max said as he smiled, backed away from the bags, and folded his arms loosely across his chest.

I looked around at my options. There were three sets of different-size bags. Each set was beautifully displayed on risers, the longer handles perfectly folded across the body of the bags. I approached each group of bags to scrutinize them. "Can I touch them?"

"Sure, sure," Max said.

I felt everyone's eyes on me as I moved from one item to the next. I ran my hand along each of the bags' fabrics, opened zippers and pockets, and lifted some of the different shapes to put them on my shoulders. I slung a smaller book bag from the canvas group over my shoulder and asked if there was a mirror.

"Oh yeah, over here." Max led me to a mirror.

The room was in quiet anticipation of a verdict. I set the bag back on the riser and looked at Mickey. Even he was quiet.

For me, it was a no brainer. "I like these bags," I said, pointing to the canvas group.

"Why?" Mickey said.

"I don't know. They just look more expensive. The leather on those looks cheap and I don't like the way the nylon is so slippery. The canvas on this one feels sturdy, and it looks cooler. I like the pockets, too. It just isn't so fussy-looking." I stumbled through my words, as I couldn't find exactly what I wanted to say. "I don't know. I would buy this bag, though." And I pointed to the book bag that I tried on.

"Cool." No snap, no point, but the word "cool" acted as a decent alternative. I already felt like I might enjoy and even thrive at this merchandising thing after all.

"Listen, you heard what *she* thinks. She's your next customer. You make the decision, but there's no comparison. Just look at how much cooler these are." Mickey had his hand on the heavy canvas bags and clearly admired the weight and "hand" (a term referring to "feel") of the canvas duffle.

Before I could register what had just transpired, Mickey was headed toward the door. "All right. Catch you later. Let me know what you decide." Just as we were walking out, the young man who had been sent to find the Kruger Park Jacket nearly crashed into Mickey as he barreled into the room.

"Here it is. The Kruger Park Jacket," he said, catching his breath.

"Unbelievable. Great-lookin' jacket," Mickey said, grabbing the fabric in his hand for a second. "Okay, thanks. Catch you later. Let me know what you all decide."

The interview was over. I was about to become the newest merchant at The Gap and had met one of the most important mentors of my life.

It was time to shed that pink suit and put on my own basic Gap T-shirt to see who I could become.

SEVEN

Making Your Mark

I was pretty sure my new job at The Gap would be a cinch and that I would immediately assume responsibility for one of the women's fashion departments. After all, Mickey had seemed impressed by my ability to spot a trend.

So imagine my shock when, on my first day, I learned my new title: merchandising trainee of Socks and Belts. With my experience and training at a top-tier company, I was, at least in my own mind, already a seasoned employee who deserved a much more elevated role, let alone a better title. *Trainee, really? And what about my keen fashion sense? What I am supposed to do with socks and belts?* It wasn't the grand entrance I had anticipated.

My very first responsibility as a trainee was the glorious task of cleaning and organizing the sample closet, the storage room where merchants kept various products and accessories as references from prior seasons. (Who knew I would put this training to use more than twenty-five years later when I was purging my Chanel wardrobe from my own closet?) Ironically, being able to take refuge in the sample closet while I learned the ABCs of merchandising wasn't such a bad place to start. Most of my new colleagues had a lot more relevant experience—having worked in Gap stores as sales associates, attended one of the big department store training programs, or graduated from schools such as FIT (Fashion Institute of Technology). They knew the lingo, the way the retail business was run, and even if they had just started at The Gap, they understood the reports and basic principles of buying and sourcing products.

But not me. I had never heard of Macy's training program, thought only farmers "worked in the field" (an expression meaning "being a sales associate"), and struggled to sew loose buttons back on to my own shirts. My preconceived ideas about this job—that I would sit around and tell everyone what products to buy—disappeared quickly, like last season's best-selling purple turtleneck. (I soon learned that a merchant is only as good as her last season.) I knew absolutely nothing about what *really* happened behind the scenes in merchandising—how products came into being, how they ended up in the stores, and what happened once they did. Merchantspeak was an entirely new language, accessorized with acronyms and strange expressions: OTB, PO, WOH, BOM, *turn* (as in how fast something sells; not a spin), *vendor* (as in supplier; not the guy selling something out of a truck), *blowing out* (as in selling well; not puffing your cheeks and exhaling), *on fire* (as in selling out fast; not in flames), *a dog* (as in a loser style; not your friendly canine). Nobody mentioned consumer research or market share, mock-ups or launch dates—the marketing dialect I'd spoken at L'Oréal. Customers weren't ignored, of course, but designers and merchants made choices in *anticipation* of their desires using something everybody call their "gut." And there wasn't a product launch every three years but thousands of new products—SKUs (stock keeping units)—sent to the stores every month.

Two months into the job, I was still spending a fair amount of time in the sample closet, trying to create order from the chaos of the past two years' assortments so we could actually use these precious archives. This particular closet bore a resemblance to the aftermath of a four-year-old's birthday party. I sorted through old piles of colored socks abandoned like deflated balloons, and belts coiled and twisted on the floor. I folded the scarves bunched up like discarded wrapping paper. Just as I was arranging bedraggled bags of all shapes, sizes, and colors scattered on shelves, I heard a faint but recognizable call: "Maureen, get down to Damon's office . . . NOW." Damon was the GM (general merchandise manager) of the Women's Division and when he called, you immediately stopped what you were doing and responded as commanded.

The Gap's merchandising floors resembled two-way fishbowls. Windowed offices lined the perimeters of the bright white space so you could see the merchants, three or four to an office, as you walked the hallways. Everyone knew what everyone else was doing at almost any time of the day. From my office, I often watched the blanched faces of other trainees as they came around the corner after having fulfilled one of the many line items on Damon's list. Other times, I averted my eyes as fellow trainees returned with the puffy eyes and red faces of those who failed to meet his demands. Now it was my turn.

All eyes followed me as I hustled to his office.

"Hi Damon, how can I help you?" I acted as chipper and friendly as I could, despite knowing that he usually didn't beckon us to exchange pleasantries. He sat behind an oversize desk that acted as a bulwark between him and his merchants.

"Where's the paisley knapsack? It should have shipped by now! It was supposed to hit the floor on eight-four!" he snapped. (Most mere mortals might say, "get in store on August fourth." I had to pause to think about what "hit the floor" meant and count to figure out which month was eight. Clearly I needed to speed up my ability to speak "merchant.")

"Let me check on that, Damon, and get back to you." I had already learned enough to know that it was better to do my homework than to whip out a random answer, especially since Damon probably knew the answer but was testing me on how well I was keeping track of our goods.

"I'll be in my office waiting." And I was dismissed.

As undignified as sample closet duty might have been, it paled in comparison to maintaining the OTB. That's open-to-buy, the inventory tracking tool, which all trainees needed to master if they had any hope of climbing out of the sample closet. Like some ancient rune, OTB unlocked the secrets to inventory management; knowing where your stuff is at every moment turns out to be one of the building blocks of merchandising. With good reason, Damon was fanatical about the OTB's accuracy. And now, with my immediate supervisor on maternity leave, I was responsible for the entire Accessories department's OTB.

I spent the rest of the day scouring every report I could find. If the bags hadn't shipped, we would miss the delivery window, which meant they might arrive in stores *after* the seasonally appropriate time to sell them. Despite an exhausting search, I still hadn't figured out the exact location of the knapsacks. I mustered the courage to go back to Damon's office.

I cleared my throat: "I wanted to get back to you about the paisley bags. I've looked at all the reports and called the DC [distribution center]. I don't know where else to find them. I need some help." I relayed my defeat in a voice just a few decibels above a whisper.

I was met with a pause that lasted several uncomfortable minutes before Damon looked up, his pen poised midair like a weapon. "What do you need, Maureen? Can't you see that I'm in the middle of something?" He pronounced each word carefully, as if I were deaf and needed to read his lips. I had no idea how to respond.

Silence hung between us for a few more seconds, and then he dismissed me with a deep sigh: "Listen, I really have other things to do here. I don't have time to teach you how to run an OTB or find your goods. I suggest you return to your office and come back when you have it figured out." With that, he bent his head back down to his work. I started to sputter something and he looked up again. "What about what I said did you not understand? Come back when you've figured it out."

As I left, I could feel warm tears flooding my eyes. I tried hard to hold everything back until I reached the safety of my office.

Crying wasn't something I did very often, but once it started, it was hard to stop. At that point, I did what any seasoned, experienced, professional young executive might do. I called my mother.

"Hi, Mom." Damn, I could feel more tears come just saying her name.

"Hi, honey, how are you? How's work?"

"Not so good. I'm just not good at this new job. I just got my head bitten off by the GM of the division because I couldn't figure out where some inventory was. And it's not that easy. They don't explain everything and then expect you to know it all." I was whimpering as I fought hard to speak. "It's so hard. I'm working really long hours but don't seem to be getting it fast enough. Besides, they give me all the grunt work, like cleaning closets and keying in purchase orders, which I know I need to do, but it's so frustrating. It's like I have to start over again. And now the head of the division thinks I'm completely incompetent. He just basically pushed me out of his office because I didn't know the answer to something." I gurgled through my tears as I told her the rest of the story.

My mom clucked empathetically and occasionally interjected with an "Aw, honey." Finally, she said, "Listen, Maureen, maybe this job isn't right for you. It sounds like you're working too hard. I hate to see you so unhappy. Do you think you should quit and find something else where you would feel more comfortable?" The pitch of her voice climbed as she pleaded with me to reconsider my position.

"I can't, Mom. I've looked all over the Bay Area for a job where

I can be close to creativity. There's nothing else I *want* to do here. And I really *like* merchandising. It's cool once you get to higher levels. You get to work with designers and pick all the styles and right colors for the stores. You go to Hong Kong to source all the materials and figure out where to make everything. I don't even mind the financial part because the numbers tell you exactly what's selling so it's like a report card on how well you chose and invested in the products. I can't quit yet."

I slowly started to pull myself together, listing all of the reasons I should stay. I wasn't going to let a tough boss get in the way of what could be my future career. I didn't like his manner, but he wasn't wrong about how much I needed to learn. I had to let go of my misplaced pride because it was interfering with my growth in this new job. Telling my mom what was on my mind and then defending my choice to stay at The Gap strengthened my resolve. By exposing me to the one alternative I had—to quit—my mom actually helped me clarify my own determination to succeed.

As for those knapsacks? Well, it turns out that finding them didn't require being such a sleuth after all. I swallowed my pride and called my supervisor on maternity leave for help. (Note to self: When in doubt, asking for assistance from the right person saves time and tears.) She gladly explained the problem: sometimes inventory would leave a factory without showing up on our reports immediately. Give it a day or two, and the inventory would show up in the system. And as for the open-to-buy? We would soon become fast and furious friends. The math was nothing more than basic algebra, and once I had learned the new vocabulary and logistics, I became as fluent as my peers.

With a renewed sense of strength, I set out to make the most of my time, in and out of the sample closet, and to figure out how to make Socks and Belts a roaring success.

❖

After my six-month stint as a trainee and another year as an assistant, I had finally become a part of the merchant "club," meaning I was promoted to associate merchandiser (still of Socks and Belts, alas) and could now rub shoulders with the "merch" managers, talk about how much I might buy of one item or another, kvetch about schlepping my samples from place to place, and share anxiety over the fearsome OTB, even if my area of responsibility seemed a little, well, let's say, random.

As a merchant, there was no escaping the necessity of fully immersing yourself in the production process and knowing every detail about your product category. While an individual merchant's knowledge depended largely on his or her category, *all* Gap merchants were expected to know the origins and specification of their raw materials, the way each item was made, and how their merchandise was finished. If you were a "wovens" merchant, you learned about the "warp" and the "weft." You understood costs per yard and you could calculate a fair "cut and sew" price, depending on labor rates in the country where the goods were made. As a knit or sweater merchant, you became an expert on gauges, yarn counts, and spinning techniques. A denim guru could describe the exact process of sandblasting and recognize a type of fabric just by the selvage. At the time, I thought it was silly to learn so many tedious details. Couldn't we just trust our vendors to provide what we needed? Couldn't they take the prototypes and copy them? At L'Oréal, we had labs, and while we spent time understanding the formulas, we weren't all required to have doctoral degrees in chemistry. But at Gap, becoming intimate with every possible influence in the process—from design specifications to the arrival of the item in stores—was considered crucial to running the business; this meant regular visits to the countries and factories that made our products.

I had already been anticipating visiting exotic places like Hong Kong, where so many of my colleagues traveled to meet our business partners. But my destiny? High Point, North Carolina, home of sock mills, furniture manufacturers, and "broasted" chicken (battered and baked, just one step away from fried). I would be responsible for checking the production of the crew socks I had ordered and ensuring our "sock wall"—the valuable real estate just behind the cash register in each and every Gap store—was chock-full of the right colors and quantities.

Crew socks: At first I couldn't understand why we sold so many of them, but apparently someone liked them . . . a lot. At the time, crews were almost 60 percent of our sock business. Many customers picked up a pair or two to match their pocket tees, enticed by sales associates who were trained to ask each customer: "Can I get you some crew socks with your tees?" It was our version of the would-you-like-fries-with-that gambit—an "add-on" purchase that, at $2.50 a pop, made it easy for customers to say yes.

Jimmy, a Long Island native and the East Coast rep for the mill, escorted me on my first visit to the site in North Carolina. He informed me that besides touring the facility, I would also need to save a damsel in distress named Amaryllis—that is, the hot pink color we'd put our hopes on for "popping the wall" (making the sock wall presentation pretty) and which was sure to "blow out." The socks dyed amaryllis were failing our quality-control tests, and the mill either wanted to ship the socks or cancel the order.

"It's crocking, Mo'," Jimmy informed me. I hadn't been called Mo since college, but I let it slide. "Not so bad really. Got a 2.5 but your mins are at 2.0. We would definitely let this one go for our other brands, but we know how tough y'all are." Jimmy's accent had taken a not-so-subtle turn South once our plane had landed in North Carolina. "The technicians dyed up a new lot. Take a look when we're down on the floor and see whether you like the new color better or maybe accept the crocking since it's just below standard. I know y'all won't compromise your quality, but you'll need to decide how you want us to proceed. We're holding a ton of greige, waitin' for dyeing."

"Crocking" could be a big problem. It meant that the color on the socks could rub off onto any fabric it touched, creating major customer complaints. But approving a new swatch with a slightly modified shade presented its own risks. Gap actually had a "color expert," Sally, whose entire job was to compare strike offs (preproduction print samples), swatches, threads, yarns, etc., against our accepted palette. Sally was the great and almighty Color Goddess of Gap. Normally the mill would have had to resubmit the new amaryllis color sample to Sally, but we didn't have time for that now. I would have to make the call on the spot. My first solo business trip, and already I had a major decision to make— one that, in my mind, held my career in the balance.

I clung to the railing as Jimmy and I descended onto the plant floor. Rows of giant cylindrical machines produced rhythmic ticking and tapping noises, the percussive sounds of what could have been hundreds of busy typewriters. We passed a workstation where dozens of women were doing something called "looping," hand sewing the seams of the socks so they'd lie flat. "We test these women's eyes to make sure they can see well enough to connect the tiny threads to each other," Jimmy told me. I started to gain a new admiration for the deceptively simple Gap crew sock. It was, in fact, the product of so many people's time, attention, and expertise—more worthy of respect than I'd imagined.

We moved past the dyeing area where large plastic bags of socks rested on trolleys waiting to be dumped into vats of color before being washed, checked again, and then tagged and packed. Finally, we made our way into an enclosed glass room full of scales, beakers, and other technical paraphernalia, like some miniature high school chemistry lab. Two men in white coats, blue netted caps, and latex gloves oscillated from machine to machine, measuring, scrutinizing, and assessing pieces of thread and patches of knit fabric. Jimmy motioned us in so I could take a look at the amaryllis samples that fell short of our quality standards.

I looked over the pink-stained patches carefully, trying to put myself in the customer's shoes . . . literally. *If I were wearing white sneakers with my pink socks and a hint of pink bled onto the edges, would it taint my view of The Gap's quality? Or, what if I sat on a white couch with my new pink socks and the color rubbed off onto the fabric?* The risk was too great.

"I know it's just under our standards, but I'm afraid I can't accept the amaryllis like this," I said firmly. The lab technicians' hands stopped in midair.

"Mo!" Jimmy protested. "You can barely see the crocked part. Let's take a look at the re-dyed lot, but honestly, I'm tellin' you, no one is goin' have a problem with this. I mean, don't forget, people don't actually rub their socks on anything the way your QA tests do. Anyway, take a look at these," as he motioned to the re-dyed samples. "I know they're slightly off standard but they pass crocking." The two technicians placed the new swatches of amaryllis under the light box.

Jimmy stood over my shoulder, barely giving me a second before launching into his next argument. "Between you and me, I would just take the re-dyed colors. It's only thirty thousand units. If it doesn't sell, it doesn't sell. Not the end of the world. We got more important things to do. The mill needs to ship; otherwise, everything's going to be backed up. But hey, if you can't accept it, you can't accept it, but we gotta problem." I admired Jimmy because he always said it like it was. While he always deferred to my judgment, his pragmatism gave me the confidence to make good decisions.

We needed this color. It was one of the key fashion statements of the season, and Jenny Ming (at the time, the merch manager in Active Wear) had bought the same color for the pocket tee. Should I risk angering my bosses by giving it the nod without their explicit approval or should I go with my own gut? I had spent a good deal of time learning all of the technical details of sock making. I could see that the new swatches were slightly too yellow according to our standard, but accepting the previous lot, with its crocking problem, would risk aggravating customers. And not making any decision then and there would back up the rest of our orders as well. It was time for me to put my training to use; it was time to take a stand.

"Okay. Jimmy, let's go with the new swatch, but next time, don't push me up against the wall with these types of decisions."

The decision ended up being a good one. I explained everything to Sally and my boss, and they praised my thorough approach. As unimportant as that little amaryllis sock might have seemed in the scheme of things, its place on the sock wall was now assured, and I had started to earn my place at The Gap, too. I was beginning to understand the impact a series of small decisions could have on the business and what impact, no matter how small my role, I could have, too. Everything I was learning, down to the minutest detail, built my capacity and confidence to stake my claim, and, when necessary, make choices that would go slightly against the grain. If I didn't want to be cleaning closets the rest of my life, I'd need to do much more than outsmart the OTB system—I'd also need to be on the lookout for new opportunities to grow the business in ways that weren't always immediately obvious. I'd have to become resourceful.

In a word: *belts.*

No one had really paid much attention to belts before I joined the Accessories department. The business had slowly shrunk to nearly nothing because our offerings were so lackluster. Thin straps made of "genuine leather" (a misnomer because it was third-rate quality) or "bonded leather" (scraps that had been ground together, glued, and resurfaced—just about as bad as vinyl) hung lifelessly from shiny, faux brass buckles. Most of the time the store's "belt wall," tucked away in a dark corner of the store, was nearly empty; most of the items had been marked down to sell at cost or less.

When I first started in the Accessories department, I loved to explore our table of belts. I'd rub the straps between my fingers to see if the leather would change color from the oils in my skin or, if it had a polish, brush the surface to feel the sheen. I would instinctually lift the strap to smell the strange tanning odor, in the same way I had watched my dad breathe in the bouquet of different vintages of wine. I seemed to have the same affinity for leather goods. What's more, I had started to notice that everywhere I looked stylishly casual people were wearing cool belts with denim jeans to finish their looks. I *personally* wanted to accessorize my own burgeoning assortment of jeans, too. As a merchant, I had to be careful not to rely too heavily on my individual taste or style to select products, but I couldn't ignore that our Women's Denim business was "on fire"—to use merchant lingo—and I was convinced that, like me, most women didn't see themselves in a braided belt (our iconic, highest-quality, and only successful style at the time). They wanted something different. I had a hunch that if we got the product right, if we improved the quality and the styling, we could sell a lot of belts.

I called Gentry, the sales rep, production manager, "designer," and jack-of-all-trades for our main belt vendor to see if we could improve our leather quality and make belts that would fit the new trends. With his flannel shirt and hiking boots, he looked more like a model on the cover of *Field & Stream* than a purveyor of Gap belts.

From his stuffed bag, he pulled out dozens of leather swatches held together by large metal rings, according to varying tanning processes and finishes. He had warned me ahead of time that none of them fit our price points, which leveled out somewhere around $9.99 after steep discounts. I coaxed him to show me everything anyway and immediately spotted one type of leather that had the perfect patina. The color was just irregular enough to give it a slightly worn-in look. The surface was neither dull nor shiny but had a kind of luster that brought out the texture of the skin. I decided to ignore his comment on price for now, figuring that if we could improve the look and styles, we would sell most of them at a much higher price and could therefore afford better-quality leather.

Next, the buckle. Most of them were men's style "harness" buckles, attractive but not the statement I had in mind for women. My eye fixed on a large C-shaped buckle made of heavy brass.

The metal had a broken-in, vintage appearance. I picked it up. Its cool weightiness indicated high quality. The round shape felt more feminine than anything we had previously carried. I held up my coveted swatch to the buckle and moved to the mirror in the office where I positioned my makeshift belt over the top button of my jeans to see if it would look good. The patina of the buckle and subtly irregular color of the leather worked in perfect harmony. *I would wear this belt,* I thought. I had the feeling it would be a best seller.

To convince Damon to approve this significant investment in a higher-priced belt, I would have to back up my instincts with some numbers. I got to work calculating how many I thought I could sell, how much more volume (a Gap term for "sales") we could do, what our potential "sell through" might be (meaning how many we would sell at regular price), and how much more profit margin we might make. I visited my friends in the Denim department to get some statistics on Women's Denim sales. My lessons in retail math were finally kicking in. Damon approved my proposal for the "C Buckle Belt," and our local factory went to work turning my hunch into reality.

I anxiously tracked our famous "C Buckle Belts" from the factory to the distribution centers and finally to the stores. The OTB and I were now thick as thieves. Every day I nervously checked my sales trend to see when it would "appear," meaning start to sell. Merchants were like stage parents, hopeful that our products would achieve stardom one day soon. We developed an intimate and emotional relationship with these inanimate objects, perhaps because we spent so much time with them from their inception. Selecting components, sourcing, negotiating pricing, and deciding how much to buy of each SKU was akin to raising children, nurturing them, and finally sending them out onstage for their debut performance. The first thing any merchant worth her salt did in the morning was to review her "trend," a thick daily report showing the sales and "turn" of each item. We were all feedback junkies, checking incessantly to see if our customers liked our dearest products.

I opened the report a couple of days after the belts hit the stores and exhaled with "YES!" It was already 4 w.o.h—meaning, at that rate of sale, we would be out of stock in four weeks. The first order of "C Buckle Belts" was blowing out! Naturally Damon had already seen the trend report, so when I rushed to his office with the good news, he looked up over his glasses with a smile: "Congratulations, Maureen. Looks like you got a winner, but"—he was quick to add—"you under-bought it! Do you know how quickly we can get back into it? You ought to give the plant a call right away to line up some reorders."

The "C Buckle Belt" established my credibility in merchandising. From that moment on, I became known for my "belt selection" prowess (if such a thing actually exists). I received kudos from the other merchants for beginning to turn around a sleeping beauty.

I was still no Dizzy Gillespie, or Miles Davis for that matter, but now that I had the fundamental building blocks under my, um, belt (and socks, I suppose)—from taming sample closets to conquering the OTB to demystifying the production process—I was able to take on more challenges. Yes, I was the associate merchandiser of Socks and Belts. I began to wear the title proudly because I'd earned it.

❖

And it paid off. I had also earned my first ticket to Hong Kong. (This is one of those cases of "careful what you wish for." Several years later, upon checking into the Shangri-La Hotel, I received a special congratulatory Polo T-shirt to commemorate my fiftieth visit.) Those trips were the stuff of legend. The "merch managers" and associates went to Asia four or five times a year and made it a point to complain loudly and often about long meetings spent selecting products, endlessly negotiating prices with vendors, and grabbing late-night dinners. Initially I took their complaints as veiled boasts meant to demonstrate the privilege they had worked hard to obtain. I soon learned the real responsibility of that privilege.

It was late one Sunday evening. We were tucked into a corner office on the twenty-first floor of one of the many nondescript, tinted-windowed buildings that lined the main thoroughfare in an area of Hong Kong called Kowloon. Long before luxury brands gobbled up every last inch of real estate in the early 2000s, Canton Road and the surrounding streets offered a colorful hodgepodge of ramshackle storefronts, restaurants, and hotels. Kentucky Fried Chickens sat next to dollhouse-size electronic shops. Peking duck glistened in the windows of small restaurants along the entrances to marble-clad malls. Bins of potent Chinese herbs spilled out onto the streets next to unauthorized watch sellers flashing blinding neon signs—all capped off at the end of the street by the terminal for the Star Ferry, which shuttled tourists and locals back and forth to Central, Hong Kong's business district. Every day we merchants would trudge from our hotel through throngs of people, weave our way around the bamboo scaffolding that encased the fast-emerging high-rises, and dodge the food hawkers to reach our office building. We worked into the evening, the air conditioner wheezing to stave off the heat and humidity, and the smells of someone's leftover lunch sometimes drifting into the room to remind us how famished we were as the meetings dragged on. We were here to review and complete our buy plan with Damon, who insisted on scrutinizing the thread color of every button and the last decimal for the cost of each purchase.

We sat in a semicircle, like obedient disciples, while Damon ran his fingers over the swatches of fabric arrayed on the floor. As he proselytized the virtues of buying 52,000 units rather than 52,500 units of a cornflower blue ribbed T-shirt, Timothy, the head of our offices in Hong Kong, burst into the room. His English was imperfect, but what he said that night was clear: "Someone left a package in the elevator. They don't know what it is but want us to vacate the premises."

Damon swung his head up, as if offended that anyone dare interrupt our important Sunday night benediction. "What are you talking about, Timothy? You're making no sense."

Timothy repeated himself, speaking a little louder this time, perhaps out of panic or perhaps hoping his increased volume would make the meaning of his plea clearer. He added, "If we don't leave soon we'll be stuck. They're going to shut off the elevators."

Damon shifted his gaze back to the floor, returning to cornflower blue as if flipping the radio station to avoid an irritating ad. Only Timothy didn't budge. He was waiting for us to mobilize. Damon whipped up his head again, his voice drenched in controlled rage. "Timothy. You can go. We're staying. I'm sure there's nothing in the elevator. Can't you see we're working here?"

The rest of us looked at each other quizzically. Were 500 units of cornflower T-shirts *that* important? What if there was really something in that package? Where's the stairwell? And finally, why is Damon insisting on staying when it's after eight p.m. on a Sunday night? An image popped into my mind. It was of my husband, Antoine, of our new home in Mill Valley, of the future we were planning together. Why wasn't I speaking up? Why wasn't anyone else? Out of nowhere, I heard the words escape my mouth. "Damon, I'm just wondering. On the off chance there is something dangerous in that package, why take the risk? I mean, you're right, we don't know what's in there, but why try to find out? Shouldn't we just leave?"

The room fell silent. No one dared to budge an inch or even look up from the floor. And yet I could feel a sense of relief and support from my peers. I had uttered what they were all thinking.

Damon glared at me as if I had planted the package myself

and then snapped back into reality, reminding us that he was the one in charge: "Let's get everyone out of here. Now!" As we filed out, a couple of people touched my shoulder, signaling their gratitude for my having spoken up.

Once we reached the elevator, Damon ordered Timothy to search the entire floor to ensure all employees made it safely to the elevator while he defiantly held the door open, refusing to leave until everyone was on board. Suddenly he was our valiant protector. I stood quietly in the corner, satisfied I had taken a stand but also fearful of the retributions for my actions.

Back at the hotel that evening, each merchant thanked me and lauded my courage. Even though Damon wouldn't speak to me for several weeks, my peers (many of whom were a level above me) now treated me in an entirely new way. I hadn't won the boss's approval, but I had gained the respect of these colleagues—not just because I had proven my mettle as a merchant but because I had shown that I had a healthy perspective on what really mattered and what didn't and was willing to risk my good standing for what I believed in. And that skill would become even more important as I became a leader. Damon ended up leaving the company a few years later, and when I took the merchandising helm at Old Navy in 1998, some of the very people in that room that Sunday night became my direct reports.

❖

So was it courage? It may look that way from the outside, but I think it was something different. Courage seems like something you need to muster or gather strength to produce for an external effect. In this instance, I didn't have time to think—I just knew what was required and I took a stand. I've never been known for boldly piping up or opposing authority without a good reason. Indeed, over the years, many colleagues have told me they appreciate that I use my voice only when I have something meaningful to say. In retrospect, I believe I stood up to Damon because I had confidence in my place at the table. I knew my business and had made something of my small opportunity as a trainee, and that allowed me to stand my ground. Speaking up, taking a stand, staking your claim—they aren't a matter of challenging authority to prove a point. Staking your claim only matters when you have something valuable to offer—a fresh perspective, a new vision, or a way of tapping into new sources for insights. Speaking up and taking a stand matter most, of course, when there is something at stake for you personally (like your life!) and for your business. It's not about grandstanding or being a hero, either. Otherwise, you're just making noise and often causing others to silence their own voices.

Sadly, too many of us have had to endure bosses or colleagues like Damon—people who use their authority as a means to intimidate you, those who make sure you know they're smarter and more powerful, those who are just not fun to work with. When faced with this kind of boss or business partner, some people bow their heads and give in; others dig in and lock horns. Neither approach seems to work out too well. Is there a better way? I've learned to take from difficult people the best they have to offer; I try to appreciate what they have to teach, without getting sucked into the vortex of their disapproval. Likewise, every professional field has the equivalent of "trainee of Socks and Belts." Making the most of even the smallest jobs helps you establish the credibility you'll need to assume bigger roles and manage larger teams later.

Over the course of the next twenty-five years, I took on a variety of assignments at The Gap and later at Chanel, some of which, at first glance, might have seemed insignificant or less prestigious than the ones I originally hoped for. But by looking beyond the label—which includes job titles and the organizational chart—I was often able to make my mark. I was lucky to have mostly good bosses after Damon, but not always collaborative colleagues. At Gap, I moved on from Accessories to Denim and eventually oversaw one of our most important departments, the inauspiciously named category of Women's Bottoms. (I laugh as I type that department name; at the time no one at The Gap batted an eye.) It was in this role that I was able to convince the powers that be to let me launch the palazzo pant, along with a number of new shapes and sizes that broadened our offerings beyond classic pleated khakis.

A few years later, I was offered the opportunity to move to a new role in a new division Gap was launching—soon to be called Old Navy. I had to decide whether to hang on to my place at the flagship division or take a leap into the unknown. Fortunately, I was still game for new adventures and learned to follow my "gut." If I hadn't been able to see the diamond in the rough, the beauty in the grittiness of real life, I would never have made the move to Old Navy. And if I hadn't been willing to take the risk of joining that hip, new concept targeting fashion-forward people unable to afford The Gap, I would never have attained the presidency at Banana Republic (a Gap company), nor would I have been scouted for a job at Chanel. Even then, I accepted the intermediary position of president of Chanel, Inc., its US division, for a two-year stint before reaching my final job. Coming from a larger business at Banana Republic, I wondered whether the scope of that role might be beneath my capabilities. But, as it turned out, making my mark running the US division prepared me to become the CEO of the global company when I assumed the role.

Long story short: No opportunity is ever too small to show you what you can accomplish, and no boss is ever so mean that you can't learn something, even if it's only to show you how *not* to lead. If you keep your eyes open, if you're willing to reframe and recast what you're seeing—yes, to go beyond the label—you'll find plenty of raw material to help you make your case.

EIGHT

Taking Charge

Mickey Meetings" were the stuff of lore at The Gap. Their purpose was to attain Mickey's approval and sign-off on the final product assortments and buy plans. The tone of these meetings ranged from wild enthusiasm to near-catastrophic despair and everything in between, largely dependent on Mickey's (and consequently, everyone else's) reaction to the products and visual displays. There was a reason that Wall Street investors and financiers called Mickey "the merchant prince"; he had a near-perfect batting average at picking best sellers. As a consequence, most merchants sat on pins and needles awaiting Mickey's discriminating judgment. Timelines were invariably tight, and decisions in these meetings could make or break a season's deliveries. Merchants and visual merchandising teams often pulled all-nighters preparing their presentations, rearranging outfits, fanning the colors of T-shirts, and organizing the look of each wall to tell the story for the season's hottest trends. Exhausted, we would then hold our breaths in anxious anticipation of that inevitable moment when our best-laid plans would be torn to pieces.

With little warning, Mickey would blow into the room, kicking up dust like the Tasmanian devil, then rush from display to display, grabbing clothes off the wall. "AMAZING!" He'd rub the fabric between his fingers. "How much did'ya buy?" he'd yell excitedly, "NOT ENOUGH, NO WAY! How many per store? How many will you sell a week? You'll be broken [out of sizes] in a day!" He'd hurl himself at the displays and, without pausing, lunge for the next item even before the poor merchant could respond. "WHAT?!? Who would buy this thing? Twenty thousand units is twenty thousand too many!" With that, the reject would be tossed to the ground seconds after the meeting had started.

It didn't matter how much strategizing we did to prepare for these meetings because you could never predict what Mickey might ask. As soon as you thought you'd figured it out, he would change the rules. For good reason—in the fashion business, if you don't change, you die. And pity the merchants who stubbornly defended a poor choice or weak buy. Mickey cut through their carefully constructed arguments in one fell swoop, homing in on exactly what customers would want and why it wasn't *this*, as he pointed at one of their painstakingly chosen gems.

Despite the pressure, I learned so much from Mickey Meetings. When you declared, "I love this pant," he'd test your conviction, point out the missed opportunities, and convince you to take an even bigger risk. I was always amazed how many merchants resorted to reams of data and comparisons to the previous year's sales figures for similar items. Mickey hated these comparisons. "Last-year-itis," he'd call it. "You can't predict the future based on the past!" And, if you felt good about how an item looked but knew its sales potential was limited, Mickey made you walk through the math of your "exit strategy"—how to preserve the highest possible margin if the item tanked. By continually challenging us to think like a customer, to put our money where our mouths were, and to hedge the bets we were placing, Mickey helped us all become better merchants.

Now as the merchandise manager for Women's Denim, one of the linchpins of our business, I was next in the lineup. What's more, I was seven months pregnant with my first child and about twenty-five pounds heavier than usual, so the idea of thinking fast on my feet was, quite literally, impossible. Come what may, I grabbed a rolling rack and, like a duck on speed, waddled down the hall to the conference room, organizing my samples as best I could. I cascaded the hangers so that the jeans were sorted by fit and quickly clipped the swatches of corresponding finishes to the jeans. I hadn't had time to get each of the finishes sampled in the right fit, which I knew would be a disadvantage. *Tough luck. It'll have to do.*

Mickey leaned back in his chair, his lips pressed together as if he wasn't entirely pleased with whatever had happened before I entered. "Come on in, Maureen," Mickey said. "Take a seat."

Tension rippled in the air. "Show us what's new and exciting. I want to see everything, even stuff you didn't buy a lot of, actually, *especially* the stuff you didn't buy a lot of." I could read between the lines. He meant, "I know you merchants don't take enough

risks, so I want to see the things you're too scared to go after because those will be our best sellers."

I'll show him I'm not afraid of risks, I thought. I was about to
unleash what I hoped would be our new secret weapon—a fantastic new fabric in a trendy new fit. Our best-selling jean was
the Classic Fit, which was high-waisted, with a straight leg that
tapered at the bottom. Personally I thought the fit was unflatter-
ing, and its declining sales indicated that I might not be alone.
I'd begun to notice wider leg, stovepipe, and even bell-bottoms
coming back into fashion.

"We have this incredible new denim from Japan," I announced.
"It's lighter weight than our Cone [a domestic mill] denim, so the
drape is amazing. And we can do it in this light, sandblasted
finish, which I think looks incredibly cool." I ignored that Mickey
generally hated when we tried to sell him on our products as I
forged on.

"Oh, this isn't the right sample. I only have it done in a Classic Fit right now, but we're going to put it into a cooler style."
My comment was met by Mickey's blank stare. A jolt of nervous
adrenaline coursed through my veins; the baby squirmed beneath my sweater.

"The mill says they have only sold limited quantities to high-
end denim makers, so we would be the first big brand to have
anything like it," I said. Was my voice cracking? "I also really
think it will look good in this new style. Our Classic Fit is really
suffering these days. I don't think cool people want to wear the
tapered legs anymore. This Stovepipe jean came from New York

[meaning from our design team, a fact I hoped would give it some "cred"]. They love it and—"

"Wait a minute! Wait a minute!" Mickey cut me off mid-sentence as he bounded back from his reclining position and motioned for me to pass the fabric to him. "This finish *is* pretty cool. How much did you buy?"

Ha, I thought. *He'll see I'm no wimp.* "A hundred thousand units in the Stovepipe jean, our new silhouette," I said proudly. "It's a lower rise than the Classic Fit and the legs don't taper but go straight down from the waist." Now I was repeating myself, as I turned to take my sample off the rack and hold it up against my burgeoning belly so he could imagine the fit. In retrospect, that move probably didn't help sell the poor jean. "Oh, this one is in the wrong fabric, but it's the right silhouette," I shot back. Mickey squinted back at me, his brow knitted, his mouth twisting in what I could only read as distaste. I handed him the jean, which he held for less than a second before crumpling it up on the table.

"No, no. How much of *this* jean?" He held up the sample of the Classic Fit and began to shake it. "How much of *the Classic Fit* did you buy in the new finish?"

Oh no. I hadn't bought *any* of the Classic Fit jean in the new finish, and the yardage for the Stovepipe had already been ordered and was on its way to the plant to be cut. "We didn't think that finish would look right in the Classic Fit, so we only bought it in the Stovepipe. I think it will look much cooler in the new fit and that's what everyone wants to wear right now." I didn't hesitate with my answer. Surely Mickey would be sensitive to what was trending and pleased that I was taking a risk on something new.

Wrong. "Wait a minute. Stop. What?!? You didn't buy your best new finish in your best-selling jean? That makes absolutely no sense!"

I'd only been head of Women's Denim for a couple of months, but wanted to show him I knew what I was doing, so I pressed on. "The Classic Fit is trending down and it really looks wrong. Women don't want jeans that taper at the ankles. It's not very attract—"

"Of course, it's trending down!" Mickey cut in forcefully. "If you keep putting your cheapest, ugliest fabrics in it, it certainly won't help sell it." Without taking a breath, he asked, "How many are you selling of the Classic Fit?" He fired the question at me. "How many are you selling this week?"

"Uh, um." I fumbled through my trend report. "Just a sec. Let me look it up." Mickey was usually okay if we didn't have an answer, but I could feel his eyes boring into me. "Um, 24,500 units this week," I squeaked.

"Okay, now how much are you selling of your second-best jean?" His voice was now several decibels louder. The answer was implicit in the question. A lot less. *Obviously.*

I couldn't resist the urge to explain my point of view one more time. He didn't seem to get where I was coming from. "We're selling four thousand units of the Wide Leg jean, but we're 'broken' [out of stock] and don't have our reorder in yet. Also, we only bought that one in two finishes and the Classic Fit is in four. I really think the Stovepipe is going to blow out. The Classic Fit is just so old and tir—"

Mickey stood up, fuming. Traces of spit formed at the edges of his mouth. All of the merchants knew that this was a very, very bad sign. His voice now boomed. "Four thousand units? And you're selling twenty-five thousand of the Classic Fit, more than six times as much? *Really?* Listen, Maureen, I gotta tell you, I am *not* going to stand here and argue with you anymore about this. You are *not* listening to me. You need to buy the finish in the Classic Fit and stop jerking around with this other thing." He flung the Stovepipe across the table and stormed out of the room. "I have to go to my next meeting."

Shaken, I gathered up my things and lumbered back to my office, sure that Mickey would fire me. I put my head in my hands and started to imagine how I would tell Antoine that I'd lost my job. Suddenly, the phone rang.

"Maureen, Mickey." *Here goes,* I thought. "Maureen, you have potential. You could be a damn good merchant. I know you have good taste and can pick best sellers, but . . ." Mickey paused. I held my breath, waiting for the other shoe to drop. "*But* you need to learn to listen. You spent that entire meeting trying to tell me you were right. You didn't hear a word I said!"

"I know, Mickey. I'm sorry. You were right," I gurgled, still trying to keep my composure.

"No," he said. "It's not about being right. And it's not because I'm the CEO. I am just asking you to stop, open your ears, and hear what people have to say. If you don't, you'll never be a great merchant. I didn't mean to be so hard on you, but I think you have a lot of potential. You need to listen better. Okay?"

"Thanks, Mickey," I said softly, suddenly realizing the magnitude of his call. He didn't have to pick up the phone or spend the time to explain to me what I should have already known. He was a busy person, the CEO of one of America's most successful retail companies. Yet he cared enough to teach me one of the most important lessons I would ever learn. To listen. To listen deeply.

At the moment I understood that if I was going to succeed, not just as a merchant but in life, I would have to practice listening; not just sometimes, but all of the time; not just to him but to my teams, my customers, and other stakeholders. More give-and-take and less defensiveness—these were the skills I'd need to develop if I wanted to continue to make my mark. Now that I had a few direct reports and depended on their input and their ideas just as much as, if not more than, my own, I was going to have to loosen the reins to become less focused on proving myself and my points and more directed toward others. Hard-charging competence and expertise weren't enough.

I also began to understand something fundamental about myself. Up until this point in my life, I'd succeeded largely because I'd been good at doing what was expected of me; I was good at winning approval—whether it was from my parents, my teachers, or my bosses. This was a way to show my worth, to stand out from my peers, and to demonstrate that I understood the rules of the game—and could play better than others. But I hadn't yet seen the darker side of this dogged determination—that it kept me in a reactive posture and could shut me off from others' perspectives and experiences. My own hunger to prove myself was overshadowing everything else, including my ability to excel at my job.

A shadow. We all have one that changes shape with our actions. Sometimes, the shadow becomes elongated and foreboding; sometimes it is amorphous and shrunken to nearly nothing. But it never disappears entirely. Psychotherapists and coaches talk about the shadow as the hidden side of our personality, the unconscious drives and desires that nevertheless inform our conscious choices. Mickey's admonitions had shone a light on one side of *my* shadow and helped me understand that I'd need to keep that aspect in check. As I continued to earn promotions over the next few years, I also learned to navigate those treacherous Mickey Meetings with more grace (and success) by seeing them as fruitful conversations and opportunities to learn from his great experience rather than trials I needed to pass. I tried to worry less about being perfect and gaining approval and more about how we might come up with the best assortment. I was able to take many of his good ideas to heart in the same way that I'd started to open my ears to the assistants and associates who ran segments of the business in my departments. As counterintuitive as it may sound, relaxing the reins a bit actually improved his and others' opinion of me. Soon, I became respected for my ability to train new hires and lead small teams.

But a few years later, when I was already an executive vice

president at Old Navy managing a team of two hundred people, my shadow started to loom large again.

◈

As a progressive company, The Gap was eager to groom a new generation of leaders to become presidents for its divisions (Gap, Banana Republic, and Old Navy), so they decided to give some of their "high potentials" the opportunity to work with executive coaches. I was one of the lucky ones chosen to be part of this effort, though I wasn't sure how lucky I felt at the time. I'd always thought that a coach was assigned when a leader was really messing up and needed a correction, like getting a trainer to reform a naughty dog. But as my boss, Jenny Ming, president of Old Navy, explained, "The coach will help you to see what you're missing to become a president." *Missing?* It sounded like yet another unpleasant test I had to pass in order to prove my worth.

When Devé, my new coach, walked into my office, I hardly thought she was the one to prepare me for my next big role. She looked to be about twenty-five years old, almost ten years younger than I was. Her athletic build and well-tanned skin indicated that she might make a better surf instructor than leadership guide. *What could she possibly teach me that I didn't already know?*

Our first meeting felt innocuous enough. She conducted a few personality tests, not unlike those dating quizzes I found at the career services office in college. (I sure hoped these would be more useful.) According to Myers-Briggs, the first test I took, I was an extreme introvert. No big surprise there. I had worked hard to "manage" my shyness over the years, putting myself in new situations and inserting my presence where necessary. It was draining, but I assumed it was the price I had to pay to accomplish my goals. Devé enlightened me with an entirely different way of seeing what I thought was a disadvantage. Being an introvert wasn't a bad thing, she explained. Indeed, many CEOs fell into that category. It just meant I derived my energy when alone or in small groups. So that's why I was always so exhausted after large meetings. Devé encouraged me to create time and space for myself to avoid those feelings of depletion. *Okay, this coaching stuff wasn't so bad if all I would have to do is take better care of myself.*

Next came values testing, where I sorted through stacks of cards to home in on what was most important to me. Devé did a "reading." *Was this Leadership Tarot cards?* I wondered. One card stood out among the rest—Integrity. "Okay, c'mon. I've known integrity is important to me for my whole life, Devé. Tell me something I don't know."

"Maureen, it's the single most important thing to you," she emphasized. I thought back to my decision to leave L'Oréal with Antoine and to my reaction to Damon in Hong Kong. In both situations (and many later) I noticed that standing up for what I believed had served me well. But I could also remember times when I had ignored my better judgment and had to course-correct. Having many peers in my age range, I naturally became friends with some of my direct reports. In one instance, I had erroneously expanded the responsibility of a friend working in my division, and soon he could no longer manage the scope of his job. His team began to complain about a lack of direction and his business started to falter. While I knew I needed to address the issue, I balked because I worried our friendship would suffer and he would resent me. I had gotten out of sync with my best sense of what was right for him, the business, and the team. Eventually I moved him into an area where he could better use his skills; he thrived and actually thanked me for taking this step. Devé explained that if I was more attuned to my values, I could be more self-aware in situations like these that threatened them; I could learn how to handle those situations more intentionally—without immediately becoming reactive or defensive. *So far, so good.*

Then came the zinger. The Gap wanted me to do a 360 Assessment to identify the "gaps" in my leadership. It's called 360 because it solicits feedback from the full circle of people who interact with you—direct reports, peers, and your bosses. It's hard to hide your weaknesses when you're being assessed from every angle, which is the point of the exercise. We see ourselves one way; others see us another. But did I really want to know how others saw me?

I wanted Devé to believe I was open to any and all feedback, but my palms were sweaty as she retrieved my results from a manila folder. "Before we start," she paused, "I just want to say: bravo! People really admire you and respect you in this company. Across the board, you're seen as a bright, articulate, strategic, and passionate leader. You are looked up to by almost all of your direct reports and peers as a great example of someone deeply committed to the company and incredibly hardworking."

"Great, that's great," I said, although I'd barely paid attention. I knew the "but" was yet to come.

"No, really. It's important you hear this part," Devé entreated. She could tell I was just holding my breath. "You have an excellent balance of skill sets—great eyes, a real knack for picking product, and also great analytical skills. You look at opportunities and know how to exploit them." I remained silent now, trying to soak up all of the nice things she was saying but somehow still unable to absorb them. "You're flexible and can course-correct when you make a mistake. Maureen, this is all really *so* great."

Then Devé dropped the bomb. "There are just a few things that I think would make you so much more effective. I mean, it's not about 'bad behavior.' These are just small points to refine so that you can continue to grow." Now, I leaned in closer.

"There were some comments from your team about how you manage them." I gulped hard. I was afraid this might be coming. Devé explained that while some felt like I was "smart and quick," they also felt like I didn't spend enough time to consider their points of view. "They love to learn from you and get your perspective but would be even more excited if you could ask them their opinions and maybe slow down enough to consider where they're coming from." Urgh. This was starting to sting a bit.

"You have really high standards, Maureen, and the team loves that. But sometimes they feel you push a bit too much. They know that you appreciate how hard they work but would love you to show it more."

Yikes. Devé had delivered the feedback as gently as she could, but I was still crushed. Why? Because it was *true*. Since assuming more responsibility with a bigger scope and much larger team, I could no longer control everything myself, which left me stressed out about delivering perfect results. I was having a hard time not showing it, too. Even though I'd vowed never to snap at people, because I'd disliked that quality in other managers, there were times when I'd lost my patience and jumped in with an answer before my team could find the right solution themselves. I knew how demanding I could be, especially right before Mickey Meetings, when I wanted to be absolutely sure that all of our products looked great and that our numbers backed up our buys. I had a hard time letting go and was always pushing, pushing, pushing for perfection when I knew something could be done better. I thought I had said "thank you" enough, but my actions didn't always match my words. I couldn't argue with the results, but I still had no idea how to fix these problems.

Devé sat calmly as I struggled to process this punishing critique. "Listen," she said. "I want you to appreciate what you do well. These criticisms? They're opportunities to do better, to build on your skills. Think of them as the shadow side of one of your talents. You are driven to succeed and set high standards. The downside is that you put pressure on yourself and on your team. Now that you see this shadow, the behaviors that might not be appreciated by your team, you can manage them, right?

Really, it's just seeing yourself from a different perspective, from how others might see you so that you refine your own behavior to be a better leader." *Seeing yourself from another's perspective.* Well, of course, that made sense. How many times had I wished Damon could see himself from my perspective? Now that I knew how my team saw me, I could work on changing my behavior to be a better boss.

At last I felt a wave of relief; I wasn't a total failure or, worse, an ogre who pushed my team too hard. My single-mindedness and determination weren't bad things—they just *were*. They were part of my personality—with both positive and negative qualities, something to recognize and appreciate but also something I'd need to keep an eye on if I wanted to bring my team along with me. Getting this kind of feedback turned out to be a watershed event for me. Before, I had always been afraid of criticism, worried that it would reveal some grave, irreparable character flaw. I had shied away from putting myself in positions that would expose potential weaknesses to the world, and those fears had been holding me back.

Over the course of the next few years, I developed a healthy respect for my shadow without letting it dominate me. And that made a noticeable difference in how I was viewed by my team and my peers. It gave me even more control, not less, in running the business. I learned to motivate others by asking questions and allowing them to discover even better solutions than those I might propose. People worked harder and ultimately delivered better results when they felt empowered. I became a stronger leader by admitting that I wasn't always right and by making it clear—and perfectly okay—that I didn't have all of the answers. This approach set me apart as a leader in the company, eventually giving Mickey and the board the confidence to name me president of Banana Republic.

But nowhere did this skill become more crucial than when I first started at Chanel and was asked, before taking any responsibility, to do nothing *but* listen. *For an entire year.* That's right. Because I was unfamiliar with the luxury business and the company, the owners of Chanel requested I move to Paris, meet the teams, learn the culture, and, essentially, put tape over my mouth for a full year before voicing so much as a light opinion. And thankfully so. My willingness to let go of my need to prove myself and embrace this silent period as an opportunity to learn (albeit frustrating, at times) helped me earn the trust of my new team members whose experience and expertise were much deeper than mine.

But if only it were that simple. Three years after I had been named global CEO, I grappled with another shape of my shadow. I sensed that some members of my team still harbored reservations, especially about the need for all of us to develop better leadership skills. They understood and endorsed the cultural changes we needed to make, but changing *themselves*? On that front they were dubious, even a bit suspicious, since they were seasoned executives with significant tenure. Having taken to heart those early lessons from The Gap, I'd conditioned myself to be highly attuned to the needs and criticisms of all of those around me. I'd spent a lot of time trying to resolve long-standing political spats, attempting to soothe wounded egos, and listening as person after person felt compelled to share their concerns and complaints with me.

Things came to a head at an offsite retreat I'd organized. We had gathered for a week of team-building exercises at a beautiful resort in Indonesia, and I'd tried to plan the week down to a tee to ensure that everyone felt safe and valued and that the exercises we did together would inspire the kind of change and new energy I knew we needed.

In a strange way, it wasn't unlike one of those Mickey Meetings. Here I was in the hot seat again, the one needing to prove myself, the one needing to have thought through every contingency and every possible question in order to prove my worth. I was hyperaware of everyone's reactions and needs. Was the room too warm? Did that person wander off in the middle of a session because he was bored? Did that other person just grimace in disgust? I felt like I had tiny sensors on my skin, constantly sending feedback about even the smallest change in mood, tone, and facial expression. And it was only day one of a three-day retreat.

As evening came, I took a walk with our facilitator, Scilla El-worthy, a renowned peace builder and three-time Nobel Peace Prize nominee. Sticky from the dense air, I swatted at the persis-tent fly buzzing around my face and the back of my neck. As the rush of the day's activities receded, I realized how exhausted I felt, as if the air were leaking out of my tires. I took a long, deep breath and tried to recap the day's exercise in as cheerful a voice as I could muster, but my words sounded flat.

"To be honest, it's been intense. It was so difficult to participate because I was trying so hard to make sure that everyone else was okay. I couldn't stop worrying about tomorrow's exercises. I just really want everyone to feel good about the way they opened up to each other earlier."

At that moment, I felt a gentle hand touch my shoulder. "You have a very loud inner critic, don't you?" Scilla asked.

I stopped in my tracks, realizing how clearly Scilla had seen me through the veneers I was putting up. I had been carrying an increasingly heavy load of responsibility, as the leader of this team—trying to encourage everyone else while beating myself up every time an issue, no matter how small, arose.

I had always considered being tough on myself a positive attribute, but bearing the burden of trying to please everyone was exhausting me and forcing me to question every decision I made—and, ultimately, straining my ability to lead. With such a strong desire to win over my team and gain their endorsements, my shadow had swung too much in the other direction: I was listening *too much* to everyone else and, as a consequence, I hadn't been listening enough to myself, which left me feeling unanchored from the vision and values I knew we needed to forge ahead. My team could see it, too—my self-doubt and waning confidence—and that couldn't help but sow further doubt among them. I'd been so focused on empathizing with others that I risked losing my way as their leader.

Fortunately, I soon found a highly unorthodox coach who taught me how to balance learning to listen with learning to lead.

❖

I'd first read about "horse whispering" in *Finding Your Way in a Wild New World* by best-selling author and life coach Martha Beck. The book explains that horses are herd animals and that, to protect themselves from predators, they seek a leader who is calm, confident, self-aware, and clear about where she wants to go. According to Koelle Simpson, Martha's business partner and equitation coach, horses react to humans in a pure, intuitive way. She explains, "They mirror how we show up. More than eighty percent of our communication is nonverbal, so these nonverbal creatures can reflect back exactly what's going on with us and whether they trust our presence and will follow our lead." Apparently, they could also expose our shadows if we were willing to work with them. Once you found yourself interacting with, leading, or herding a horse, you learned "in your body" how to show up differently, how to be attuned to others without losing touch with yourself or your goals. I decided to go to Martha and Koelle's ranch to find out for myself.

Martha, who earned a PhD in sociology from Harvard, is a slender woman with a strong and wiry frame. Her energy is kinetic, and her voice crackles with intelligence and sharp insights. In contrast, Koelle, just over thirty years old, seems gentle, almost soft-spoken and timid . . . at first. Her youthful appearance masks fifteen years of experience in equine coaching; her strength comes from a place of stillness and calm and from her deeply intuitive understanding of equine *and* human behavior.

Their ranch is tucked into a forest of deciduous trees. As soon as I stepped foot on the land, my senses sprang to life. My nose tickled from the smell of warm mulch. The soft breeze ushered in sounds of whinnying from a distant pasture. I noticed every twig and blade of grass as if seeing for the first time. I sensed something big might happen.

On my first day, I watched Koelle work with one of the horses in the ring. From the first moment she strode into the ring and the horse immediately stood at attention, she demonstrated what it means to be attuned to others while leading with confidence. Koelle slipped her arm around his neck, petted his nose, gave him a kiss, and started walking as if on some important mission. Without any hesitation, the horse followed. Now it was my turn to step into the ring. "Just, just do whatever you like," Koelle insisted. This was the extent of her instructions.

Staying as still as possible, I fixed my eyes on the tip of the horse's nose; puffs of steam from his moistened nostrils hung in the air for a split second. *Remain calm, focused. Act natural,* I told myself, taking in the earthy smell of the morning dew and damp sawdust. I had read that horses sense inauthenticity as soon as a person steps into the ring and generally ignore such pitiful souls, so I wanted to show the horse how comfortable I was and that he had nothing to fear, that my intentions were good. I figured that if he could get used to my presence, he would allow me to come near and hopefully let me lead him. *See, I am patient, gentle, and kind. I am not going to bother you. You can trust me. I promise.* That's what I wanted my body to convey to him, but despite the chill in air, I could feel a small bead of sweat trickle down my spine. I gripped the lead line tightly as if it were my last friend in the world; my hands were starting to go numb, my knuckles white at the tips. I shivered aloud and saw his ear twitch just slightly. *A good sign*, I thought. I took a couple of timid steps forward, my heart in my throat as I made my way to touch his mane.

As I approached, he bent his head as if beckoning me to give him some affection. *Ah, so you* do *like me*, I thought. *We're going to be swell friends.* Feeling bolder, I mimicked Koelle's move, wrapping my arm around his neck and bringing his head close to my face. Either he really liked my attention or was using my face to scratch the side of his cheek, because the horse began to nudge me and rub against me just a little more aggressively than I anticipated. I tried to keep my balance, caressing his nose with my opposite hand, whispering sweet nothings into his ear. He continued to push his wet nose into my neck. I pretended to ignore the slobber from his mouth now staining my light tan nubuck jacket. I thought it was sweet . . . kind of. Actually, I was getting a little nervous about how assertive he was and started to pull away.

"Great, Maureen. See, he's really comfortable with you." Koelle's encouragement came from the bleachers above the ring. "Now, why don't you try leading him a little? Just decide where you want to go and start moving in that direction."

I took a few steps and, to my surprise, he followed right behind me, so close I could feel his hot breath on my neck. I picked up my pace a bit to create some much needed space between us, but the hairs of his nose now tickled the back of my neck. I kept walking, beaming from ear to ear that I could lead this baby on my very first try. *I must be an excellent leader,* I told myself. *Even the horse knows it.*

Thunk. I lunged forward a little. *Thunk.* The horse was shoving me with his nose. I jumped out of the way and let out a little screech; I was afraid he would knock me over. Something wasn't right.

"Maureen, Maureen." Here was that sweet voice again. "Is this what you want the horse to do?"

"Um, uh not really," I said, dodging the oncoming horse. "I mean, I think he likes me, but he's getting a little too close. How can I get him to stop pushing me?" I was alternatively cowering, ducking, and gingerly pushing the horse's head away from me.

"Tell him what you want him to do." I knew the horse wouldn't really respond to verbal cues. *So what the hell am I supposed to do now . . . mime?*

I set out again, this time determined to keep the horse at bay. When I sensed him coming too near, I instinctively threw up my hand in a stop-sign gesture and he backed away. Four or five steps . . . stop sign. He stayed close but kept a comfortable distance. We walked. Another four or five steps, he started to move in, and I flashed the stop sign. We continued. This lasted for almost a full turn around the ring. I started to regain confidence; I'd found the trick.

"Great, Maureen. That's it. Really nice." Koelle's voice was still encouraging but firm. "Now, I want you to do the same thing without your hand." *For God's sake,* I thought. *I'm finally getting the hang of this thing. Why does she have to change the rules?*

I looked up at the bleachers with a questioning gaze. "Show him with your body," Koelle said. "Tell him with your posture that you are in charge and capable of leading him. Show him you know where you want to go."

I breathed in deeply, squared my shoulders, and planted my feet firmly into the ground. I looked straight ahead and began to walk. As before, the horse followed, but this time, when he started to invade my space, I felt myself get a little taller. Instead of moving out of the way, I stood my ground, directing my gaze in his direction to show him where my boundaries were so that he wouldn't nudge me. Although my moves lacked the subtlety of Koelle's, I'd found my own distinctive way to lead this horse. I wasn't imitating her or anyone else, and I also wasn't overthinking and overanalyzing every step, as I'd sometimes done as a leader. I was just doing what felt right—and it was working.

"That was excellent," Koelle said after I'd made a few turns of the ring. "How did it feel that last time, once you got the horse to keep his distance?"

I was out of breath. My heart was pounding. "It was really cool, exhilarating," I said excitedly and took my seat on the bench.

"So what did you learn?" Martha's blue eyes had been on me the whole time, even though Koelle had done most of the talking. "Seems like you may sometimes have issues with establishing boundaries, no? Did you find that the horse's behavior might have been a little like any of the people you manage?"

Damn. How the hell had she picked that up from just watching me with the horse? It had occurred to me in the ring that my problem with the horse might just reflect some of the issues I was having as a leader. So worried about being accepted and admired, I sometimes had a tough time holding my own space. Listening had helped me develop deep relationships, but at times like that offsite retreat in Indonesia, I let all of the feedback overwhelm me and forgot to listen to myself.

"You're right, it was," I agreed.

"So now you'll know what to do when it happens. You see, what just occurred in the ring, you actually felt it, didn't you? Could you *feel* what happened in your body when you became aware of your own state, focused on grounding yourself and standing tall? Everything changed for you and the horse felt it, too. And he responded to your power."

I thought back to my earliest meetings and interactions with my team at Chanel. It had been a little bit like this first experience in the ring—the horse breathing down my neck as I tried to lead him forward. It was only at times when I was able to give myself a moment to decide what *I* thought was right, where *I* thought we needed to go, that my team quelled their complaints and requests and started to get on board. I'd had to recalibrate the dynamics of that relationship and I'd had to learn to trust my instincts to tell me what felt right. The more I did that, the more successful we'd all be.

I subsequently brought two Chanel executive groups back to Martha and Koelle's ranch to share this remarkable experience. I noticed that each person had a different approach, reaction, and relationship to the horse that reflected his or her own style and challenges. When someone tried to mimic another's successful moves, the horse immediately sensed inauthenticity and ceased to interact. No matter who you are, the horse teaches you to operate from a place where you are centered and grounded in your own authentic state of being.

❖

When you first start out in your career, it's easy to think that leadership is about being bold and decisive and about calling the shots. But once you actually become the one in charge, you realize that the role is a complex and a deeply human endeavor. Positional power and titles—taking the corner office—only gets you so far. The real authority comes when you are able to strike the right balance between empathizing with the needs and desires of those who follow you *and* having the confidence to set the conditions and the tone for getting things done. It can be hard to resist the temptation to spend your time getting everyone to like you, especially for women, but that's not sustainable—nor is it the point. In order to lead—and to get anyone else to follow you—yes, you do need to listen to others . . . a lot. But you also need to be attuned to yourself—your hungers, your drives, and your trigger points. In other words, you have to manage yourself in order to lead others.

You don't need to do an offsite retreat in Indonesia or to train a horse to listen more deeply or seek feedback. Both are practices you can cultivate on your own and with those you trust to provide you with an adequate mirror. And as for knowing your intentions and sense of direction: I have found that taking a moment to move away from circumstances where you might feel pressure or triggered—to ask yourself what's most important to you underneath the surface—helps restore your equilibrium.

Your shadow may not be the same as mine. As Devé said, one's shadow is often the flip side of one's well-honed strengths. So what do you do well and how does that unique talent manifest its darker side? What might that mean for how you behave in your job or in your life and how can you adjust to improve? When are you possibly overshooting and losing your way?

Shadows never really disappear, but they don't have to color everything you do. We can practice new ways of being and move past old patterns that prevent us from achieving what we truly want. We are all, always, a work in progress.

NINE

Having It All

H i, Dad. I need some advice." I had just been offered a promotion to divisional merchandise manager of a new company Gap was setting up (what would become Old Navy), and I wasn't sure whether I should take it. I was ready for more responsibility, and there were no positions open at The Gap, so joining this start-up offered the most upside. The risk, of course, was that if the new venture failed, I would be out of a job. "Sounds interesting," my father replied. He was a man of few words. But when he did speak, his comments always seemed to get to the crux of the matter.

When I was a kid I would watch my dad play gin rummy with himself. He would lie on the bed and deal two hands, putting one facedown and then switching back and forth to play both sides. As a lawyer, my father was comfortable with contradiction and conflicting emotions and motivations, and his method of considering all sides of a situation had been invaluable to me whenever I'd faced important decisions in my life.

It was a habit I'd started as a teenager, when I sought his help with homework assignments. On any given night, I would enter his room through a billowy cloud of cigar smoke and ask him questions while he simultaneously watched the Cardinals on TV, listened to another baseball game on the radio, and worked on the *New York Times* crossword puzzle, pen in one hand, cigar in the other. My father possessed an unusual mystique. He hated small talk, but at cocktail parties he could often be found off in a corner, where a small group of people had been drawn to him. They sought his opinion on various topics of the day, which he offered scrupulously and sparingly. He was more interested in absorbing the world around him than in making pronouncements about it, and I am still amazed today by the range of his knowledge and interests. When I would ask him how in the world he knew so much, he'd just shrugged, lowering his heavy eyelids, with an "I dunno."

But it wasn't just *stuff* he knew. He also had an uncanny way of tapping into and teasing out people's core motivations, whether they were buried deep beneath the surface or elevated above the radio waves of normal conversation. And when he finally spoke—after listening carefully to your answers to his pointed questions—you felt privileged to hear his reasoned, precisely modulated responses. Sitting next to him on the bed, I hung on his every word, hoping someday I might be just like him, so thoughtful and articulate. Meanwhile, I was fortunate to be able to seek his advice once again as I considered my next career move.

My mom offered a different kind of support that has been equally important during crucial moments of my life. When I was growing up, she devoted herself wholly and unequivocally to my sisters and me. She spent every waking hour keeping us clean and well-fed but also supplying us with endless affection and compassion as we explored our dreams. She set up my guitar and piano lessons, tirelessly drove me around to friends' houses, took me shopping for the newest trends, and made a healthy three-course meal at night. She helped me through my teary-eyed breakups and cheered me on in my first challenging year at Burroughs. When I was in labor, she flew in from Saint Louis to be with me. And in each and every mini-crisis, I called my mom, just to hear that reassuring and warm cluck, "Aw, honey."

Both my parents seemed to love their jobs and the roles they played for my sisters and me. You could say that my upbringing looked pretty traditional—certainly for the '60s and '70s—with a dad who worked and a mom who didn't. My father reveled in his work as a lawyer and still does at the age of eighty-two. And my mother is proud and gratified by her "investment" in raising her daughters while enjoying a vibrant social life full of tennis games, theater outings, and bridge tournaments. I never intended to reproduce their model in my life with Antoine, but I've been able to take a few pages from their approach. Seeing my father engaged with his work influenced my own wish to pursue a career and eventually become a leader. It never occurred to me that I wouldn't work. In fact, it never occurred to me that I wouldn't support myself financially and contribute to supporting a family. It just seemed obvious. But I also always assumed I'd have and raise kids. My mom's pleasure and satisfaction in seeing us blossom, her full love and kindness in helping us grow up, inspired me to want to do the same for my own children someday.

I never questioned that I could "have it all," at least not until I had to confront the reality of what it means to actually have it all—to have the experience, that is, of having *all of it* coming at you at once.

❖

Long story short, I ended up taking the job at Old Navy, when the company was still only an idea being hatched by a small team trying to figure out how to make it work. About a year and a half after our initial store opening, business was booming. Customers at our 150 locations were clamoring for more—of everything. Our famous "Item of the Week" T-shirts, shorts, and tank tops vanished within days of hitting the shelves, as did our Performance Fleece tops and Painter's Pants. Desperate for our cheap-chic clothing, customers snatched up the packages, shrink-wrapped like supermarket fillets, right off the back of the 1950s Chevy pickups parked in the front of the stores. They stood in long lines zigzagging down the wide aisles, their black mesh bags overflowing with our low-priced, hipster styles. We were unstoppable, which also meant there was no stopping the incredible workload required to keep up the pace. As vice president of the Women's Division, I was sorely understaffed and treading water to keep from drowning in my new, increasingly challenging managerial responsibilities. Oh, and I was pregnant with my second child. Our first daughter, Pauline, was just over two years old, in that period fondly known as the "terrible twos" where the smallest incident could create the storm of the century. I frantically tried to get home each night before she went to bed so I could see her latest tumbling moves, watch her "pretend read" *Madeline*, and smother her in kisses.

Up until this point, Antoine and I had mostly shared parenting duties. His job at a soft drink company and later as a consultant didn't demand as much travel or as many late hours as mine did, so he could be present at home when I couldn't, which allowed us to minimize the use of day care and nanny hours. I still managed some of the household chores like cooking—not Antoine's favorite task—but for the most part, we'd found a groove that worked and that gave me the confidence and peace of mind to be able to throw myself fully into work.

Having gained upward of thirty pounds during my first pregnancy with Pauline, I was determined to stay more fit with this one, so in addition to my hectic work schedule, I started my mornings around six a.m. at the Bay Club, either swimming a mile or training on some instrument of torture like the Versa-Climber or stair stepper, and often ignoring my ob-gyn's advice to keep my heart rate under 125 beats a minute. I'd hit the office by eight thirty or nine a.m. and cram down some quick oatmeal while studying the data from the weekly trend report before our staff meeting. What was selling? What was slow? What should we chase? What was a dog and ready to be marked down? From the staff meetings, I jog-trotted through my day: first to a gathering in the cubicle-laden area in front of Jenny Ming's office, then to a best-seller meeting, next to a buy-plan meeting, then to a visual merchandising walk-through, an advertising meeting, a Mickey Meeting, and finally an Item of the Week meeting. The days rushed by at a breathless speed. I was lucky to grab a soggy salad while reviewing some product assortment with one or more of my merchants. By seven or eight at night, I dragged my exhausted, depleted self home just in time to put Pauline to bed, broil some barely edible fish or chicken for a hasty dinner with Antoine, and then collapse in bed by nine, lulling myself to sleep with repeats of *Seinfeld* or *Will and Grace*. It was exhausting, but it was also an exhilarating time. When I stopped to think about what we were achieving at Old Navy—taking a start-up from nothing to a runaway success in a period of a few years—it was hard not to want to give it everything I had.

At a routine checkup in my seventh month, my doctor suggested an ultrasound, because I wasn't gaining weight fast enough (no surprise, given my strict workout schedule and slapdash eating habits during those adrenaline-fueled workdays). The perinatal doctor and I made small talk as he glided the wand over my gel-slicked belly. He fell silent as he circled the wand over and over the same part of my abdomen.

"Well, the baby seems healthy, but you're losing amniotic fluid," he concluded matter-of-factly. "Normally, your levels should be much higher."

A slight panic set in. I knew I hadn't been taking good care of myself, but wasn't I too strong to have any *real* issues?

"For now, everything's fine," he said, "but you'll need to come in every week for an ultrasound until you're at term. If your levels drop much beyond where they are today, we'll have to put you on bed rest until you reach term. Drink lots of water, stay off your feet, and get more rest. Otherwise, you'll put the baby at risk."

That last sentence gave me pause. It was the first time I had fully appreciated that there might be consequences to my insistent exercise regime, long hours, and stressful workdays. Regardless, I checked my watch, hoping to get back to the office before dusk and wondering how I would fit weekly doctor's appointments into my jammed schedule. I had still failed to see the seriousness of the issue, thinking that I could control my body and that work stress would in no way affect my physical condition.

For the next three weeks, I forced myself to go to the standing appointment with the perinatal doctor. On my fourth visit, there was no small talk. "You need to have this baby right away," he said, so coolly and seriously that I felt as if I'd just been shaken from a daydream.

"So, does that mean I should check into the hospital in a couple of days?" I still couldn't believe there was any real problem. My previous work experience had taught me to take nothing at face value and to push hard past any resistance to get the answer I wanted.

"No, it means I want you to check in *now*." The doctor's tone was compassionate yet firm. "Call your husband to get your clothes and drive yourself over to the hospital. There will be a bed waiting for you there. I'd like you to have the baby tonight."

"Tonight?" I was in a complete state of shock. What would

I tell my boss, Jenny? We had a Mickey Meeting on the following Monday. I hadn't reviewed all of the buy plans yet. I hadn't worked with Visual Merchandising to set up the room. I wasn't ready! But obviously, this new baby had different priorities.

In my hospital bed that evening, I waited with Antoine for the contractions to start. The Pitocin (the medicine given to induce labor) didn't work right away, so I had a restless night, mostly lying awake, praying that the baby would be on her way without a problem, and kicking myself for not being more careful over the last several months. Suddenly my body experienced a kind of internal explosion with the force of a rocket surging from a launchpad. Then, with no pushing and almost no effort, my beautiful and healthy baby girl, Mimi, burst into the world.

Overwhelmed with relief, I regretted allowing my work to take charge of my life. Could I have worked out less, come home earlier, worried more about my health and less about my business? Would Old Navy have grown as fast and as far if I had slowed down? There's no way for me to consider this incident without a tinge of remorse.

I decided to slow down a bit—well, let's say I *tried*. I took an extra two weeks of maternity leave—beyond the official six weeks provided by the company. Instead of rushing back to the office, I sometimes held merchandising meetings on my back porch so that I could still be with my infant. I tried to organize my travel so that the whole family could be together on weekends. Without much discussion, Antoine now took on all of the household tasks in addition to much of the child rearing. But as time went on, even this model turned out to be unsustainable. As my work responsibilities increased, so did my need to be available to my team and in the office to handle whatever might come up. At the same time, Antoine hadn't gained as much traction as he had hoped for in his consulting practice.

Worried about our finances and the impact that having a full-time nanny would have on our relationship with our kids, we made the joint decision to change the form of our family existence entirely. Antoine left his job to take care of the kids and work from home. Strangely, it wasn't a major conversation or catalytic event but rather a natural evolution of our roles and a pragmatic choice. Between the overhead expenses for Antoine's consulting business and our nanny fees, it would cost us more for Antoine to work in an office than from home. The buoyant stock market and online investing had also started to pique Antoine's interest, so he decided to devote his time to managing and investing our finances—work he could do while juggling the kids' school and activity schedules.

Our choice, while more common today, was less so in the mid-1990s, and we didn't immediately have any role models on which to draw, except for a few colleagues at The Gap. The idea of "mister mom" was still a source of ridicule and contempt, as was the concept of women being career-minded executives. Not surprisingly, making the decision to go beyond the label in creating a family life that worked for ours was easier than dealing with the external pressures and expectations others directed our way. At times, I was shunned by the stay-at-home mothers in our community for not joining after-school get-togethers or weekends at Jumping Jacks (a toddler tumbling class). Antoine endured the snide comments of his family and friends who feigned acceptance of our unconventional model but still held tightly to the belief that "a woman's place was in the home" and a man's at the office. Neither of us paid too much heed; we had already disavowed the traditional labels, satisfied with our own way of being spouses and parents. For us, the decision itself made perfect sense and suited each of our sensibilities.

Even so, my priorities often seemed to be in conflict with one another. I still dreaded leaving on a business trip any given Sunday night and worried my absence might have a negative impact on the lives of my precious girls. One night while I was overseas, Antoine rushed Mimi to the hospital with a urinary tract infection; I kicked myself for not being there with her, too, and for not having seen the signs sooner that something wasn't right. And then there were the more mundane but equally significant daily events that I often missed: the funny new words they'd learned as toddlers, the first time they'd swum without blow-up arm wings, their grade school "graduations," their playdates. I missed so many everyday moments that poignantly marked their lives. I wished I could have had more time to read them bedtime stories and tuck them in at night or drive them to school in the morning and pick them up in the afternoon. I wished I had held their hand at dentists' appointments and brushed their hair for school portraits. As hard as it was and as guilty as I felt, I never allowed these feelings to subsume me entirely because I trusted Antoine's loving care and knew that when I was home, I could wrap them in my arms and give them every minute of my attention. So for the most part, we were all happy. Antoine enjoyed playing mom and dad, I was thriving at work, and the kids seemed satisfied.

Like many of the well-organized moms in our community, Antoine signed the girls up for everything from swimming to horseback riding lessons, from Tae Kwon Do to ballet. He attended daytime recitals, afternoon concerts, weekend swim meets, and after-school matches, often befriending other parents in the audience and on the sidelines. In the morning, he packed lunches, in the afternoon he went grocery shopping, and in the evening he gave the girls their baths. And in "all" the time in between, he figured out how to refinance our house and invest our savings. His diligence and mind for logistics made my life after work feel effortless—well, sort of. When I did make it home on time, often exhausted and sapped of energy, the kids were clean, usually fed—Antoine eventually learned how to put a piece of salmon in the oven or spaghetti in a pot—and ready for snuggles. Even during vacations, Antoine arranged fun activities at every moment of the day so I could recover and enjoy quieter downtime with the kids. Once they grew older, our roles shifted to adjust to their changing lives. Antoine still did much of the logistical work, but I became increasingly involved with their education and social lives. I helped with schoolwork where I could, talked through spats with best friends, shared time at the movies, and swapped favorite books with both of them. In this way, the role I played with my daughters wasn't all that much different from the role my mother had played with my sisters and me. Pauline and Mimi developed a natural understanding of who did what; "Papa" made sure they could explore what they loved and got to where they needed to go, and Mom offered advice and compassionate understanding of the trials and tribulations of being preteen and teenage girls.

Some might say I had the best of both worlds—a vibrant career and a stable, happy family life. And I am truly and deeply grateful for the life I've been able to lead. But it wasn't perfect, and it wasn't balanced in the way that phrases like "work-life balance" would have you believe. Both Antoine and I had to make compromises and sacrifices as husband and wife and as parents; we gained some things and gave up others in an attempt to find the roles that delivered the best possible outcomes in an imperfect world. Were our expectations of ourselves and each other always reasonable? Were they always met? Well, no, especially when we got caught up in trying to conform to standards and labels set by others. And even when we did buck convention, the impact of our good intentions wasn't always immediate or obvious. Look no further than your children to make it perfectly clear what your limits are, as my older daughter, Pauline, did for me as we prepared to send her off to college.

❖

We were starving. Pauline and I had spent the entire day trudging around Harvard's campus, listening to the stump speech of our handsome-jock tour guide touting the many virtues of this esteemed institution. I remember his emphasis on the eclectic and "artsy" student body, the open and accepting social scene, and the diverse and unusual academic offerings. This was our fifth or so college tour, and we had become familiar with the routine. At Harvard, they emphasized that, contrary to popular perception, much of the student body did not go on to business, politics, or law. Yeah, right. (As a Yale graduate, how could I possibly say anything nice about Harvard?) Regardless, Cambridge had a plethora of interesting restaurant choices and I'd chosen Oleana, a Middle Eastern eatery that won high praise in Zagat for its large selection of vegetarian choices. At sixteen, Pauline had declared herself a vegetarian and had strict—no, closer to draconian— rules about where we might grab a bite.

The restaurant was buzzing. My eyes followed the plates of mezze spinning by, balanced on the arms of acrobatic waiters, as we headed to our table. "Oh, that looks good, doesn't it?" "Wow, check that one out." "I can't decide what to get. It all looks amazing."

Pauline didn't answer. Was she annoyed by my giddiness? She was always very reserved and played her cards close to her chest, which I understood, an introvert myself. I was accustomed to having to ask a series of probing questions before she might give me more than a one-syllable answer, but tonight something seemed even more awry. Pauline was in a particularly unpleasant mood, perhaps irritated at me for subtly (or not so subtly) pointing out the reasons that she shouldn't like Harvard. I immediately ordered a glass of wine to ease my nerves.

I don't exactly remember the genesis of the argument or the precise words that ignited the flame, but what began as an innocent spark, rather like that one random cigarette thrown out of a car window, suddenly burst into an all-out forest fire. I vaguely recall wanting to taste Pauline's dish and when I sensed her reluctance, I had made a sarcastic comment about how little she liked to share with me. This clumsy critique must have triggered some deep resentment, because without any real warning, Pauline began to attack my parenting skills.

"Well, you were never there for me, anyway . . . ever. Daddy always took us everywhere. How many soccer games did you come to? One? You were always on a plane, going to Hong Kong, to France, wherever. I don't even know how you can criticize *me* for anything! You never even spent any time with me, and now you're telling me what I should and shouldn't do and how I'm supposed to act. You have a lot of room to talk!" For someone who wasn't normally loquacious, her words burst like flames from her mouth. Her pent-up hurt and anger exploded into a blaze of seething condemnations.

Blood rushed into my face, the tips of my ears turned bright red, and my scalp started to itch, but it wasn't from the fiery spices in my food. Hunger stalled, my tongue seemed to swell in my mouth. I couldn't swallow another bite. I sat across from my older daughter, my baby, my love, unable to utter a word.

It was true. From her perspective, I hadn't fit the version of a good mom that most of her friends had. Just six weeks after giving birth to Pauline, I'd been on a plane to Asia, where I continued to travel intermittently (along with many other destinations) most of her childhood. It had been her father, not me, cheering her on from the sidelines of countless sporting events. I had always prioritized academics and showed up for school conferences, awards ceremonies, and meetings with advisers because that's how I thought I could contribute the most to my daughters' experiences. (Antoine, being French, knew less about the American school system.) But when I did, the other mothers with whom Antoine had made friends regarded me with incredulity, having assumed, perhaps, that I was only a figment of my poor husband's imagination.

And to make matters worse, my job with Chanel forced the family to relocate to Paris when Pauline was only eleven. During her most delicate and socially sensitive years in grade school, she'd had to start over, find new friends, and engage in a new life in Paris. Pauline loved the outdoors and reveled in the crisp, clear weather of San Francisco's Bay Area. She considered our move an undeserved punishment. Never having lived in a city, she dreaded waiting for her school bus on dark rainy January mornings, and she bemoaned the strict French methods of teaching at the international school she attended. As beautiful as Paris is, the city can be unfriendly to children, who are often seen as nuisances in boutiques or finer restaurants. (It was more acceptable to bring a dog to dinner than a child.) The urban life—replete with busy streets, irritated drivers, rows of buildings, however majestic, and a lack of sufficient playgrounds—roiled Pauline's sensitive soul. She'd spent many a miserable night crying herself to sleep. How many nights had I held her as she wept, unable to say anything other than, "We'll be home soon"? Not soon enough, according to Pauline.

I could feel the warm tears well in my eyes as I took in the profound significance of what she said. I bit my lower lip and looked around the restaurant, trying desperately not to burst out crying. The lump in my throat was about to choke me.

I'd always worried that Pauline might feel neglected. I'd beat myself up on more than one fifteen-hour plane ride for being a "bad mom." I'd sobbed in my hotel rooms after hanging up from a late-night conversation where she forgot to say "I miss you" back. But I'd managed to convince myself that Antoine's exceptional presence filled in for my inadequacies. Pauline had never mentioned her disappointment to me, never insisted I attend any of her events, but I now realized that her shy and reserved nature probably obscured much of the pain she had felt. Now, in this moment, it felt as if my world, my choices, everything I'd worked for had crashed down on top of me. Not able to wait a second longer, I popped up from the table, scrambled to the restroom, and broke down.

It was a long time before I could regain my composure. The guilt filling every pore in my body gave way to the first blushes of self-pity. What could I have done differently? If I hadn't worked so hard, we probably wouldn't be touring a college like Harvard. Why couldn't Pauline see that I was working for her and the family, too? It all seemed so unfair. Anger, remorse, sadness, self-disdain, blame. Conflicted by so many opposing emotions, I made my way back to the table. On the one hand, I was secretly hoping that once Pauline saw my puffy, red face she would apologize or at least allow us to return to a more mundane topic. On the other, I yearned to apologize myself, to lay my heart on the table and try to explain. But when she just stared past me into the distance, I shut down, consumed by even greater feelings of remorse.

Of course, different kids have different personalities and different needs. Mimi, more extroverted, requested me more, insisted that I show up more for our shared interests—she loves to read, go to theater and movies, pursuits I also enjoyed. Mimi's overt requests were helpful; if I didn't go to her horse shows enough, she'd let me know it. Pauline, with her quieter personality, wouldn't let me know what she needed—until she finally did—and then it was hard for me to hear, let alone know how to address. I'd tried to show up the best I could, but I knew deep down that I wasn't showing up as much as she wanted or needed. Pauline was right. I had to take that in fully. I had to own it, meaning I had to own the mixed bag of feelings those decisions had generated: both pride in my professional success and guilt for not being more present with Pauline.

I hated seeing Pauline so hurt. In that moment, I could only feel her pain and my own incredible sadness at having caused it. I could only beat myself up for everything I didn't do and all the ways I hadn't shown up. I couldn't recognize, understand, or see anything I might have done right as a mother. What *did* I give my daughter? Did my presence positively contribute to and impact her life at all?

Ironically, three months prior to that unfortunate trip with

Pauline, the National Mother's Day Committee had conferred the title of "Outstanding Mother" on me. I wore a cream, open-neck Chanel suit to the awards ceremony. Mimi, then thirteen, accompanied me, looking adorably chic in black ballet flats, leggings, and a silk white and yellow dress. Pauline had already started her summer job and was unable to attend. I regretted her absence, but I was proud of her resolve to begin work as soon as school was out. As I posed for photos next to the other recipients—Dr. Holly Atkinson (award-winning physician and author), Alfre Woodard (actress and political activist), Victoria Reggie Kennedy (lawyer and widow of Ted Kennedy), and Mindy Grossman (CEO of HSN [Home Shopping Network])—I felt ambivalent. We were being honored as "exceptional women for successfully building their careers, nurturing their families, and helping improve the lives of others." I could vouch for building a successful career—I was exhilarated by the work I was doing at Chanel. But I'll be honest; even before the incident with Pauline, there had been so many times when I felt I'd flunked as a mother. Should I feel good or guilty? Could I truly say I deserved being called "Mother of the Year"?

As women who want careers, we often feel we should also fulfill all of the parenting duties society specifically assigns to the "good mother," on top of our demanding jobs. And because none of us is superhuman, we often lead exhausted lives trying. Because of these preconceived ideas about what it means to be a "good mother," we might also feel limited in asking or demanding that our partners play a less conventional role to allow us to pursue careers. Even when we do go against the grain and redefine our parenting relationship, as Antoine and I did, we will inevitably experience moments with our children that cause us to question these decisions.

I'm fairly sure that I wasn't the only prizewinning mother that day who was silently asking these questions or grappling with these issues. What working woman doesn't worry that her children will suffer for her professional gains? What working woman doesn't wonder what professional opportunities she'll lose if she does decide to devote more time to home life? What working woman hasn't tried, if only temporarily, to figure out the perfect formula for having it all? If only we could find the right solution, right?

Wrong, it turns out. There is no perfect formula. Sadly, there is no perfect balance to be had. Whatever you choose, there will be both happiness and sadness, both positive and negative outcomes, both pride and guilt—and, most likely, all of the above at once. Perhaps that's what it really means to have it all—all of those competing priorities and conflicting emotions, all at once.

❖

A few months after we completed our tour of prospective colleges, I found myself sitting on the floor of Pauline's bedroom, papers strewn in every direction, the computer casting a blue glow on her angelic round face.

"Mom? What should I write my college essay on? I'm stuck." She was belly down, her elbows bent, head in hands, and her beautiful green eyes staring up at me.

I could feel the warmth in the center of my chest. Pauline wanted my opinion! Even though we'd never formally resolved our earlier spat, here she was telling me that she valued my advice. We batted around different themes until she realized how much she loved the notion of community and family, and began to craft an outline that could reveal this tender side of her personality. In the end, she thanked me and hugged me.

And I thought for just a moment, maybe, just maybe, I hadn't been that much of a train wreck of a mother after all.

Did I still feel guilty about my intense commitment to work and not being there at times she wished I was? Yes, and I still do. But this incident caused me to reflect deeply on who I had been as a mother to my older daughter and on who I had been as a parent, at all. As I looked back on our relationship over the years, I realized that even though my travels kept me away from home a lot, I had shown up when she needed counsel. I might not have followed her day-to-day activities as much as Antoine did, but I *was* there to provide her a comfortable home and a good education. When I was home I was present to provide a warm and loving embrace, a shoulder to cry on, a mirror to reflect in, or even a convenient place to file complaints. And today, not much has changed. Both my kids know that they can rely on me to provide solid ground when they need it. I gave Pauline some of the things—the things I knew best how to give—that she needed to become the beautiful, smart, and centered human being she is today.

And even though I imagine she still harbors some pain regarding those times I wasn't there, she also appreciates our continually evolving relationship. During Pauline's four years at Yale (#sorrynotsorry, Harvard), I was invited speak to the students about Chanel, my career, and my life. And each time I came, not only did Pauline attend but she brought a posse of friends. She beamed with pride at dinners when her friends listened to the story of my career and asked questions about how to manage their first jobs. From time to time, she still sends me articles about the struggles for women in leadership, and she has been actively and curiously checking in with me about writing this book. After graduating college, when I helped her to find her first job, she made a funny comment to me. "Mom, you never really did much ironing or cooking—even if I do love your apple pie (one of the only five dishes I have mastered)—but in the end, I much prefer having a mom who gives me career advice and helps me get a job." In so many ways, I am a role model for her, even if, at times, a flawed one. Pauline is now pursuing her own path, uncovering what feels right for her and what will bring her the most joy. Having been told, like so many undergraduates, that her degree in art history will get her nowhere, she carried on, soaking in the beauty and subversive nature of her major. Thanks to a deep passion for nutrition and the process of bringing healthy food into the world, she worked for four years at the Yale Farm and upon graduating found her first job in a company making pure, untreated products back in her beloved San Francisco.

❖

So back to those questions: How do you achieve work–life balance? How can you "have it all"—your dream job and a family? What's the trick?

The trick is . . . there is no trick. I haven't had it all, but neither has Antoine. We figured out how to work together so that we could each play a significant role in our children's lives. We each made certain compromises and adjustments according to *our* circumstances and what *we* each could offer. These circumstances, strengths, and desires are different for everyone. There is *no* one right way. There is not one label you can slap over your family and call it perfect.

It is the labels themselves that can make these choices even more difficult. We still tend to *assume* that women should bear more of the parenting responsibility than men even when we wholeheartedly pursue careers. If we don't unpack these assumptions, if we don't stop and ask why it is so, we just end up exhausted and discouraged.

But what might happen if we throw off the gender straitjacket, move beyond these labels, and encourage parents to define their own models, ones that best fulfill them, fit their circumstances, and provide for their children? No one can have it all, but what we can all strive to have, men and women alike, is what we *want*. No, not *all* of what we want but what we *most* want. The real "trick" is understanding what it is you *do* actually want and being clear with yourself and your partner on how you both want to lead and prioritize your lives.

How to get to what you most want? By letting go of definitions others might set for us as well as the idealized images we may have created ourselves. I had to let go of the way many of my neighbors and friends defined "good mothers." Similarly, Antoine let go of a conventional career trajectory and of the staid definitions others had of "being a real man." We also had to unhook ourselves from the ideals of perfection and embrace the inevitable paradoxes of our lives—all of the fulfillment and disappointment, the happiness and sadness, the gains and losses. By releasing ourselves from these restrictions, we have a shot at creating success on our own terms. None of this is easy, but it makes for a helluva more interesting life.

TEN

Soul Calling

Between 1994 and 2000, Old Navy's business soared, reaching its peak, with just around eight hundred stores and $5 billion in sales—a record-breaking, meteoric success by all accounts. Unfortunately, business had started to move in the opposite direction for the Gap division. Its precipitous decline had coincided rather inconveniently with the growth of its less expensive sister brand. Some observers were sure it was due to a lack of exciting product. Others swore it was Gap's oversize real estate "footprint" (lingo for "too many stores") and their aging fleet. Still others chalked it up to lackluster advertising. But everyone seemed to agree that Old Navy's fashionable threads, quirky ads, and industrial chic store design had taken a chunk of Gap's business. Wall Street was nervous, the board of directors a little rattled, and the teams inside the division in frantic turmoil to turn the namesake division around. For a while Old Navy's success made up for the shortfall and kept the wolves (of Wall Street, that is) at bay. Temporarily.

Just around the start of the new millennium, while the Gap division continued to flail, Old Navy's business also began to take a dramatic plunge. After months of negative double-digit comps (comparative store sales—the year-over-year metric used as a benchmark of business health), this decline could no longer be attributed to poor weather or any other convenient excuse. Some critics postulated that the clothes had become too young: skirts too short, pants too tight and full of extraneous details, shirts too fitted. Others claimed that the once humorous ads had become stale and tired. Many thought the innovative store model—low-rent boxes (retail shorthand for "stores") in strip malls that required more and better service to handle the volume of customers—needed to evolve. And most lamented the revival of brisk competition from Target and Kohl's and the arrival of global fast-fashion retailer H&M. No matter the reasons, everybody blamed Mickey.

I was now the EVP of Old Navy merchandising, planning, and production and was poised to present Old Navy's new fall collection to the Gap board of directors, hoping it would mark the beginning of a turnaround. I paced the halls and went in and out of the conference room while I waited, adjusting a pant here and a brightly colored fleece top there. They were nearly five hours late. What was the delay?

Sullen. Nervous. Distracted. They finally arrived, filing in one by one. Some board members' eyes darted around the room, pretending to take in the clothing in front of them. Others swiveled their necks mechanically back and forth like bobble heads, their vague half smiles barely hiding their discomfort. Mickey, his head bent low, had shoved his hands deep down into his pockets.

Something was wrong. It just wasn't like Mickey to simply stand there, motionless.

"Should I start?" I looked around. Only five of the board members were there. Mickey glanced up for a second, caught my eye with a remote gaze, and returned to his deep contemplation.

"Sure," the lead board member muttered. No one was paying any attention even though their bobble heads had all bounced toward me. "Is this the new fall assortment?" He'd barely noticed that we stood in a room chock-full of colorful clothes.

I launched into my well-rehearsed soliloquy. "Our turnaround strategy really focuses on balance. The last several seasons, we tried to tone down the product to gain back our core older customer, but I think we really swung the pendulum. Nothing got better. We heard from the customer that the assortments were boring, lacking color and details." I was desperately trying to grab the board's attention, which seemed to have wandered off. I looked over at Jenny Ming, puzzled as to how to proceed given Mickey's utter silence and the board's obvious preoccupations. She gazed at me with a stilted but defeated smile that said, "Just keep going."

The lead board member finally piped in. "So, you guys still believe in Performance Fleece?" Ah, he was throwing me a bone. *I got this one.*

"Yes!" Words started tumbling out of my mouth excitedly. "We think we could double our sales in Performance Fleece. We have some fantastic new silhouettes this year, like this full zip jacket for men's, women's, and kids'." I began to pull the rich heather brown sample off the wall to show off the pockets, the contrast inside neck, and the striped bungee zip pulls.

"Great, great," said one of the board members as he ran his hand along other clothes on the wall, looking off into the distance. "So, what else is new?"

Huh? *The whole assortment was new.* I caught Mickey's eye again. He just shrugged his shoulders.

"Well, we have this incredible new heavy-weight canvas pant for men and boys. The hand is super soft but you can feel how sturdy it is." I started to pass around the sample.

The lead board member finally decided to put an end to the farce. "Okay, Maureen, Jenny, looks great. We gotta run. Back to the board meeting. Sorry we were so late. Assortment looks strong. Great." And they filed out.

I barreled into Jenny's office, where I found her with her elbows on her desk and her chin cradled in her two hands as she gazed out the window. *Unlike Jenny,* I thought. She always had the spunk and dynamism of the Energizer Bunny. (She would often arrive before dawn, spend a full day in back-to-back meetings, go home to cook a gourmet dinner for her family, help her kids with homework, then bake cakes, cookies, and pies for the team for the next day.) I rarely saw her in this meditative pose.

"Mickey's been canned. I can feel it," I whimpered. "Did you see him in that meeting? He didn't say a word! He never does that. He didn't even look at the product!"

Jenny got up from her desk and sat next to me, taking her tea mug as if she might need it for extra balance. "You think so? I'm not so sure. They would have told me."

"Jenny!" I had a hint of alarm in my voice. "C'mon, that was *not* normal. The board didn't give a crap about anything I was saying. They barely looked at me or at the clothes."

Jenny smiled with lips sealed and nodded. "Yes, it was strange. I don't know. Maybe they're just stressed about Gap's business. Their comps are worse than ours and I just saw their fall assortment."

"Oh really? Was it bad? God, when are they going to figure that thing out?" One of our favorite topics was discussing what a disaster The Gap had become. As bad as Old Navy's business was at the moment, theirs was always worse and their decline had started long before ours. Misery loves company, especially when others are even more miserable, I suppose.

After several minutes of comparing notes, I left her office. A storm was brewing.

The next day I was called into Jenny's office. "Close the door," she said as she sniffled, her eyes red and puffy.

"I knew it!" I shouted. "They fired him. Goddamn it! What the hell? How could they? They're such idiots! Okay, business sucks, but really?!?"

Jenny started to gurgle something—she rarely got angry and never raised her voice—but instead grabbed a Kleenex to blow her nose.

"Seriously?!? Don't you think he made them rich enough?" I ranted. "Damn."

Jenny could barely talk. "You need to get to your office. He wants to talk to you, too. I just got off the phone with him and they're calling us all into the boardroom any minute now."

I could feel myself start to tear up as I hustled to my desk to wait for Mickey's call.

"Hello, Maureen. Mickey." Gravely, nasal and soft, his voice was unrecognizable at first. And then, silence. I could hear him swallow in the background. "Um, uh. I have made the decision to leave The Gap." His voice cracked.

I didn't know what to say. "Okay," I whispered, warm tears filling my eyes and overflowing onto my computer keyboard. "When? Right away? Why?" I didn't even care about the answers to my silly questions.

"I don't know. A few months. I'll be here for a little while during the transition." There was a long pause while he covered the phone, feigning a cough to hide his sobs. His scratchy voice came on again. "Yeah, I guess it's just time for me to go. I did as much as I could."

"I'm sorry, Mickey. I am so sad. I loved working with you." The words seemed so juvenile, but it was the best I could do. My heart ached. Through fourteen years of our infamous Mickey Meetings, he'd taught me everything I knew about merchandising. He was the soul of The Gap, the life force, the shining beacon for all merchants and designers, for anyone creative, really. He had been tough on me at times, but fair. He trusted me and believed in me. Even when he vehemently disagreed, he treated me with sincere respect. I was losing more than just a teacher and inspiration, more than "the greatest merchant in the world." I was losing a mentor and a friend.

"Okay. I gotta go. We'll catch up later. You're one of the good ones, Maureen. Take care." And Mickey hung up the phone.

❖

Twenty, maybe thirty execs lined the boardroom that sat on the top floor of our brand-new building. The room was filled with latent anxiety. Most of the execs didn't know for sure why we were there, but given the request for a 12:35 meeting (after the opening bell of the New York Stock Exchange), most guessed it was grave. The entire room fell silent when Don Fisher, the founder and chairman of the board, entered with Mickey behind him.

Don walked awkwardly to the head of the table. His bushy eyebrows peeked up over his big square glasses and seemed to weigh heavily on the tops of his eyelids as if he were forever squinting. He put his hands in his pockets. "Good afternoon. We have an important announcement to make this morning. I will give the floor to Mickey."

Mickey's face was swollen and red as he unfolded a piece of paper he gripped in his hand. "I have just informed the board"—he began to sniffle and choke—"of my desire to resign as CEO of The Gap." Now tears were streaming down his cheeks.

"I joined this company nineteen years ago and since that time we have all built a tremendous business. I am proud of what we have been able to accomplish together and want to thank you for all of your hard work, devotion, and support." At this point, Mickey was outright bawling.

The room was dead silent except for the soft sobbing of the execs who loved Mickey so dearly. I stared into my lap. I'd never seen a man cry this way and certainly not one of the stature, strength, and aura of Mickey Drexler. His vulnerability reached in and squeezed my heart. I could hardly breathe as I felt his pain and humiliation. Mickey had poured every cell of his body into the business and into energizing the people he led. He may have been tough, even erratic at times, but only because he cared so profoundly about the brands and individuals who managed them. We all knew the truth; he'd been fired. The board had lost patience with him as the business spiraled downward and his radical attempts to change course continued to fail. (Ironically, business started to improve shortly after his departure thanks to many of the changes he had initiated.)

Don Fisher read a bland, monotonous thank-you to Mickey for his years of service as if it were a necessary checklist, filled with empty qualifiers like "creativity, passion, and vision" to demonstrate his "admiration" while Mickey continued to bawl.

We all filed out of the room silently, some stopping to hug Mickey, others squeamishly finding the door. As I took the elevator down to my office, the absurdity of the scene hit me. Here was perhaps the greatest merchant ever, a visionary leader who literally invented The Gap as customers came to know it, who created Old Navy, and who transitioned Banana Republic from safari gear to a hip, modern brand. Here was a man who combined the best of every quality needed to run a business and lead a team. Here was a man who'd shaped and trained more great merchants than any other person in retail, who had opened their eyes wide to the beauty of the world and allowed their hearts to lead their choices. And after everything he'd done, he was brought to his knees, reduced to a list of empty platitudes.

Mickey's firing was seared in my memory, creating a scar that helped guide me to where I would go next and what kind of leader I wanted to be. His contagious energy and enthusiasm, his unwavering love and passion for the product and those who created it, and his respect for the customer, not as a number or statistic but as a real person, left an even greater imprint. Since his departure in 2002, The Gap has cycled through three new CEOs; none has managed to turn it around entirely. They lost many of the great merchants and design talent who once drove the company's success. I often wonder what might have happened if things had gone differently, if the board had found a more inventive way to benefit from Mickey's genius, and if the pressure from The Gap's shareholders hadn't forced Mickey's severance. It all turned out better for Mickey, who went on to reinvent J.Crew. But in the end, when a company loses its heart and soul, it also loses its best talent, and eventually its raison d'être.

Speaking of raison d'être, now what was mine? Prior to this cataclysmic event, I had been eager to take on more responsibility. I felt ready to articulate my own vision for a brand and yearned to lead a business end to end with all of the functions, from finance to design, reporting to me. And of course, I expected recognition for my past successes; after all, I had been part of the team that had grown Old Navy from the ground up. I was ready for a bigger title with more money—I wanted to be a president. Without a position available other than at the Gap division (which was too big, complex, and mired in politics), I started answering the many calls I'd been receiving from recruiters, thanks to Old Navy's stellar performance. I developed a healthy policy of listening patiently and answering politely—you never knew when you might really want to talk to a headhunter—but they all deployed the same rhetoric. Some nameless but highly successful company was looking for someone with "exactly the kind of experience you have." I passed on most of the offers I received because I wasn't inspired by the CEO, the location wasn't right, or the company's products left much to be desired. I was still committed to succeeding at The Gap.

Only one call, from Heidrick & Struggles, the preeminent headhunting firm for high-level execs, intrigued me. You never turned down a call from Heidrick because they were known as best in class, rarely recruiting for any position under a president or C-suite search. I was a possible "match" for a "French, privately held luxury company" whose name absolutely could not be divulged for confidentiality purposes. It didn't take long to guess the identity of this mysterious stranger, the *only* wholly privately held French luxury company: Chanel. They wanted to meet me but were in no hurry to fill a position that apparently didn't yet exist.

Thus started a series of intermittent interviews, lasting well

over a year, with the owners, other recruiters, and various executives at the firm. It seemed they were intent on getting to know
me . . . on their own time. (I later learned the expression used
proudly but sometimes frustratingly by Chanel teams, *"le temps
Chanel"*—Chanel time, which was determined by the House, not
by objective metrics such as minutes, hours, days, or months.)
One high-level executive whose title remained a well-guarded secret only asked me a couple of business questions, mostly about
what it was like to build a brand, how had I led the teams, and
what happened during Old Navy's decline. I was puzzled that he
didn't ask the classic interview question: "How did you drive your
business?" He wanted to know more about how I viewed Chanel
as a brand and, specifically, how I might treat it and approach
working there. My second interview was with someone whom I
would learn later was *the* key decision maker at Chanel; nevertheless, we spent most of the interview talking about my family,
my love for France, and where I liked to vacation. Each time I
tried to ask questions about the size of the company, the scope
of responsibility, their ambitions or organizational structure, I received vague and generic answers. *What kind of company was
this? When could I brag about helping to catapult Old Navy from
zero to $5 billion? Or did they even care?*

I didn't hear back from Chanel for months; I imagined I had
not met their expectations and eventually put my curiosity about
the discreet and elusive brand on hold to pursue my quest at The
Gap. Upon the strong advice of a friend and a mentor in finance,
I mustered up the courage "to ask like a man"—meaning "not

underselling myself like a woman" (his words) by explaining why I was qualified—to become president of Banana Republic. In the final weeks of Mickey's six-month transition out of the company, I was awarded the position, though I couldn't help being annoyed that I'd had to resort to a masculine power move to get it done.

The challenges of the business fascinated me. Like a cat with many lives, Banana Republic had survived several eras and multiple mutations. Starting as a safari-inspired store in the late 1980s, the brand drew in hordes of customers with its well-designed, multi-pocketed travel pants and photojournalists' vests. Faded antique maps of faraway places lined the walls next to piles of well-worn, sturdy khaki and olive trousers. But once customers had their stash of lion printed scarves and Crocodile Dundee hats, the stores looked more and more like sadly aged theme parks on markdown. Business slumped. Thanks to a savvy marketer (Jeanne Jackson, hired away from Victoria's Secret) and a herd of consultants, management discovered in the thicket of customer research something called a "white space" (a term meant to describe a business opportunity) in the contemporary market, an unfilled desire for "accessible luxury." That insight in the late 1990s ushered in a whole new look for Banana Republic and a temporary resurgence. Sleek, slim suits, sparsely decorated leather bags, and crisp white shirts breathed new life into the company. Stark black-and-white photography, orchids, and contemporary Italian furniture replaced the faded maps, swinging vines, and pith helmets of the original concept. Crowds of yuppies, metrosexuals, and wannabes fawned over the faux Prada mannequins posing with aplomb in the freshly painted black-framed window displays. Unfortunately, when the skinny pants trend failed to appeal to less sculpted customers, down went the Banana Republic business once again. The "Prada" years had come and gone, and Banana was yet again in search of a new personality.

What a great new challenge for me! I had cultivated an intuitive sense for brand identity when we created Old Navy and knew I could upgrade the product. I was ready to practice everything I had learned—from Mickey, from Jenny Ming, and even from the earliest days at L'Oréal when James had shown me how an image can speak to the heart of a customer. Only I had never actually *run* a full business end to end. I had never had so many direct reports, many of whom had more experience and longer tenures. I had never been exposed to the Gap board without the safety net of Jenny's reassuring and motherly presence. I had never had twelve thousand sets of eyes watching my every move and waiting for my vision and guidance. In my own mind's eye (no one actually requested this of me), I had ninety days to come up with a plan, twelve weeks to show the board I was worthy, and three months to inspire and pump some ambition into my new team. I would have my work cut out for me—all of this while figuring out how to work with The Gap's new CEO.

Lean, tan, with glowing green eyes, Paul Pressler, Gap's new CEO, immediately wooed the board, the market, most of the teams, and even me. His genteel manner and bright smile reassured us, even the most skeptical of Mickey fans, that he would continue to sponsor and support our creative and merchandising efforts. But as time went on, I learned he had a slightly different way of viewing what the French might term as "*le nerf de la guerre*" (literally, "the nerve of the war"; figuratively, "the heart of the matter").

You see, up to this point, designers and merchants played the leading roles in the company, conceiving innovative products, and selecting and investing in trends. Together, these two teams predicted the future by creating desire, usually before customers knew what they wanted. All other functions supported this delicate dynamic, which favored "gut" over analysis and strategy. Paul, having come from a more traditional marketing background at Disney, hoped to buoy The Gap's analytical and strategic skills. Forget Mickey's rallying cry, "Buy it like you love it!" Paul strongly preferred that merchants make product choices based on consumer research, profiles, market segmentation, and "white spaces." He sought to redistribute organizational power, giving as much weight to planning, production, and financial concerns as to product creation and selection, which had long ruled the roost. And for good reason, Paul also sought to improve efficiency since The Gap's profits were in a slump. As the company had grown, so had the number of employees, often overlapping in their roles and responsibilities. He hired consultants to streamline our activities. His moves were textbook marketing.

I agreed that a little more rigor might help us identify the right customers—especially at Banana Republic, where our schizophrenic identity could use some focus. And we did need to invent new ways of working together to optimize our talents. So I tried to learn the new language of bar charts and graphs, customer segmentation and "white space." I memorized terms like RACI (responsible, accountable, consulted, and informed) and worked to apply "organizational fitness" models to my team. I revisited the material from a previous executive education course at Stanford—a kind of "Finance for Dummies"—and reread acclaimed business professor Michael Porter's theory of "unique activities" to ensure my brand's strategic differentiation. I pored over classic management books and even subscribed to the *Wall Street Journal*.

To no avail. This was not a language I was meant to learn. I never liked geometry, didn't take any math classes in college, and, working in the notoriously unpredictable fashion business, I had shied away from relying too heavily on analytics. I started to have nightmares about triangles, circles, squares, and diamonds. And by now, you definitely know how I feel about boxes. In my experience, clients don't fit into neat little categories, and they cannot tell you what fashion they might want a year ahead of time. Asked to tuck away my intuition in favor of grids, charts, and grafts, I started to feel I might not be the right "character" in Paul's reimagined "magical kingdom." I remember going to one of my first "Paul Meetings" while at Banana Republic, showing a gorgeous navy men's cashmere coat of which I was particularly proud, and being asked, "Can you describe the kind of 'guest' who will buy this jacket?" Paul quickly corrected himself to say "guy," but you get where I'm going. My soul was melting.

That's when the recruiter for Chanel called back to fly me to New York. After months of silence, my enigmatic prospect wanted to get to know me even better.

I *was* intrigued, not to mention flattered, and even honored that such a reputable French brand might still be considering me for what I finally learned was to be the top spot—global CEO. Coincidentally (or perhaps not!), I had just met, was stricken by, and purchased my very first Chanel jacket during one of our European "inspiration trips." At The Gap, when business was good, you got to take two trips a year to Europe; these were shopping expeditions where you'd buy samples, take pictures of interesting displays, and study different ways of merchandising. Mickey believed these trips would help us cultivate our "eyeballs" (merchantspeak for "taste level"), refine our "guts," and hone our intuition about what trends and styles might catch on with our customers. On this particular trip, I visited a hip store in Paris called Colette when I spied her—yes, the jacket was most definitely a "her"—hanging in the Denim area. I fell madly in love. Up until that point, I had never dared enter a Chanel boutique for fear the sales associates might scoff at my Converse sneakers and cargo shorts. I had never considered Chanel a brand for me, as it seemed both financially out of reach and perhaps a shade too conservative and subdued. But seeing this jacket in such an ultramodern store completely changed my previous misconceptions (more proof of the deconstructionist theory of context and subversion). The cream and brown tweed and denim jacket styling paired perfectly with my own jeans. I shrugged on the jacket and visited every mirror in the store, trying to justify the astronomical price tag. I walked out of the store empty handed but continued to stalk that jacket in each and every Chanel boutique in Paris until I knew we could not live apart. I finally returned to buy her at Colette because she looked cooler there, mixed and matched among their more casual threads. I had a hunch that I'd stumbled along an important new trend. *If Colette's getting these jackets*, I thought, *Chanel's going to be hot again.* As a merchant, these observations always meant something, even if knocking off a Chanel jacket at any division of The Gap was a long shot. But this time, I wasn't buying a sample for business purposes. The jacket was for *me*.

◈

I had no idea what to expect when I took the elevator up to the forty-fourth floor of Chanel's New York offices and was confronted with picture windows framing the most expansive view of Central Park I had ever seen. Peering down at the tiny sunbathers, hot dog stands, and horses and buggies, I stood awaiting my next rendezvous. I looked up at the giant portrait of Coco Chanel and felt terribly out of place. I had a moment of wondering if there were two "me's"—the one who hung out at the shopping mall in Mill Valley on the weekends in torn jeans and Birks, without a stitch of makeup, and the one now nervously smoothing over the wrinkles of her serious gabardine suit while imagining that her lipstick might be getting crusty. Would I really fit in here?

As strange as it may sound, I wasn't entirely sure I *wanted* to join Chanel at this point in my life. Having spent almost fourteen years in the Bay Area, I felt like The Gap was the center of the universe, the *only* place to be. Up until The Gap's Great Decline, we had the pick of the litter for merchant and design talent and my successful run at Old Navy promised a solid career trajectory for me. Of course, I knew the rags-to-riches story of Chanel's famous woman designer, remembered admiring beautiful ads starring Catherine Deneuve for the Nº5 fragrance, and had seen photos of its current designer, Karl Lagerfeld. But working at Chanel, much less leading the company? That's not something I'd ever imagined, and yet it had started to make perfect sense.

It was more than just the chance to speak French again or work for a luxury brand. Something else kept me engaged in imaging a future together, despite my many unanswered questions and Chanel's lackadaisical interview process. When I met various Chanel executives, they seemed to care about less obvious things than the issues I'd grown accustomed to hearing about in the boardrooms of The Gap and L'Oréal. We didn't spend time discussing business plans or processes. I didn't see one chart or graph. While they eventually shared some business results, they seemed infinitely more interested in how to balance their eighty-year legacy with modernity and how to grow while preserving the exclusivity of the brand. Many spoke of Coco Chanel's story, her vision as a woman, and of the incredible importance creativity played in everything they did. For a girl who loved beauty, I couldn't help but be intrigued.

The recruiter said I'd done well with the interviews that day, but when several more months went by with no word, I assumed the position had gone to someone else. Then, nine months later, I received yet another call, inviting me to fly to Paris for an additional interview. It was a "formality," I was assured—this time with a small French recruitment firm. Their offices exuded the highest degree of French aesthetics and good taste: tall ceilings capped with refined moldings, herringbone floors glowing with a honey-colored patina, the minimalist décor signaling effortless chic.

"Entrez," my interviewer entreated and invited me to sit in an Eames chair directly across from her. I felt her study my outfit—a brand-new Gucci pin-striped pantsuit I had purchased just for the occasion. (I figured it might be too soon and too presumptuous to wear Chanel.) Clad in a simple Prada suit, she cracked a short, closed-mouth smile of approval. (I later learned that Gucci was one of her other clients.) Soon the quick pleasantries and polite demeanor gave way to intense questioning.

Many of her inquiries centered on how I saw creativity. Did I believe marketing or the creative side drove the business? How did I work with design teams? Did I tell them what to do or did I allow them lead? At the end of our conversation, I was completely exhausted, but her insistent questions had given me another glimpse into the values of my potential new employer. She was speaking about image, about beauty, and about exceptional product. *Was it possible that they spoke the same language and cared about the same things I did?* Perhaps my lack of experience with luxury brands wasn't as much a disadvantage as I'd thought. Perhaps my love of beauty and creativity were what really mattered.

After such a prolonged courtship, I was both surprised and excited when Chanel finally decided to make me an offer. I was just waiting to receive their employment contract when I learned there was one more test I'd have to pass. Chanel had asked that I meet with a corporate psychologist for a final assessment.

❖

Back in New York I walked up the broken concrete steps of a dilapidated brownstone and rang the bell to the office of the man I'll call Dr. Nounours. *Thump . . . thump . . . thump.* The door creaked open. "Hi, come on in, we'll be on the second floor." A large man shook my hand and motioned toward the stairwell. "I'll take the elevator. Bum leg. It's the door on the right. Just take a seat and I'll be there in a minute."

As soon as I opened the door to his office, I saw them. Pink. Most of them were shades of cotton candy or bubble gum. They occupied a lot of space in the tiny apartment, randomly placed on mostly empty bookshelves, atop the refrigerator in the adjoining kitchen, stuffed inside the open TV cabinet, tucked into the corner of the L-shaped couch, and even perched on the narrow glass shelf of the bathroom. All different shapes and sizes of mostly pink teddy bears, a kind of fluffy jury, I suppose, ready to pass a verdict on my final test before being hired by Chanel.

I took in the cramped apartment and my fluffy new friends, still unconvinced I was in the right place. *Was the man with the bum leg Dr. Nounours? Was this his "office"? And if so, why were there pink teddy bears everywhere? Were they part of my test? Would he be judging me based on how I reacted to these unusual circumstances?*

After several minutes, the doctor arrived and introduced himself. He held out his hand again. "Sorry about the wait. It takes me time to move around." He collapsed heavily into the chair next to me at a round table. "The Chanel folks asked me to get to know you a little. So really, you can just relax, be yourself. We're going to have a conversation. No reason to be nervous."

The rest of the five-hour appointment remains mostly a blur. Dr. Nounours did indeed engage me in a conversation peppered with questions and obscure "what if" scenarios. "Imagine you were in a library, studying for a test, and someone sitting next to you makes a lot of noise. What would you do?"

Why was Chanel interested in my studying habits? "Well, I would probably get up and find a quieter spot, I guess."

The doctor started to write something down. *Did I answer that okay? What did that say about me?* "Let's say there are no other spots around." He pressed on. "Then what would you do?" I obviously had not completed the response.

"I would probably try to ignore the noise, I suppose." He looked me straight in the eyes, paused, and then once again scribbled something on his paper. *Was he driving at my conflict management skills? What on earth did this have to do with quilted handbags?*

"But let's say they are really loud and you can't concentrate?"

Oh my God, when will he stop? Am I passing or failing? "Okay, okay. I would probably politely ask the person to quiet down." The questioning continued until after several hours, he handed me a written exam. After I completed it, he asked me to write something in French.

"What do you want me to write?"

"Oh, anything you would like. It's just for a handwriting sample." He lifted a complicit eyebrow. "You know, the French. . . . They believe you can assess someone through their handwriting. I have nothing to do with this part. Trust me. I just need to hand it off to them." I almost laughed, wondering whether the teddy bears agreed.

As I reached for my bag, ready to leave, Dr. Nounours had one last question on his mind. "So, you're probably wondering why I'm so fat?" I sat back in my chair, in a state of shock. *How on earth does one answer that kind of question?* I went through a couple of possible answers quickly in my mind.

"No, I didn't notice." Can't say that—it would obviously be a lie. *"Yes, what's wrong with you?"* A little too bold and not very sensitive. I finally settled on looking him deeply in the eye and waiting for him to continue. He told me how he'd hurt his leg, how it left him both depressed and incapacitated. I listened intently and expressed my sympathy for his situation and my hopes that his recovery would be speedy. I felt we had connected on a deeper, human level.

When I researched him later, I noted his sterling reputation and understood why such a sensitive company might call on his services. Indeed, the entire interview process—beginning a year and a half before and culminating in this unusual exchange—revealed as much to me about my new employer as it must have revealed to them about me. The company I was about to join was infinitely more interested in what kind of person and what kind of leader I would be, how I might treat their loyal employees, and how I would think about preserving the brand and taking it into the future. So many CEOs prove their worth by making sweeping and rapid change, forsaking the past for what they believe will be a brighter future. This was not what Chanel was looking for because it wouldn't serve the brand, whose heritage was truly unique and inspirational to women around the world, or its people, whose exceptional talent and loyalty had nurtured the brand over time. They wanted someone with a deep understanding and respect for its legacy. This delicate balancing act would require keen observational skills to understand the evolution of the world paired with introspection to delve into the core essence of the brand and mine the gems that might have been overlooked. It would require deep listening to garner intelligence from its highly seasoned and tenured employees along with respect and love for the creative process to foster innovation and see beauty in disruptive ideas. Equal doses of humility, pragmatism, and confidence would be prerequisites, too, as would patience, lots of patience to make thoughtful, measured decisions in a world that often pushed us to go fast. Patience and humility would be especially important as I was about to spend three full years of training before taking on my full responsibilities. The first year I would move my family to Paris and spend each day just *learning*, without being responsible for any defined meetings or objectives and without any staff or even an assistant. If that first year went as planned (or *unplanned*, as it were), then I would spend the next two years "on the ground" in the operational role of the president of Chanel, Inc. (the US arm) before assuming my position as global CEO. Despite Chanel's approach—or rather, *because* of it—I was able to see how the company's values fit with my own.

Obviously the hard facts—salary, job title and position, location, and scope of responsibility—matter a great deal, as do the "softer elements"—organizational culture, chemistry with your new boss and peers. But making career decisions is never as simple as running through a checklist. And it's not even always logical. In fact, just before accepting the offer from Chanel, I almost betrayed my intuition and accepted another position from a company whose "upside" (meaning ability to make more money) looked much more attractive. Luckily I was able to backtrack and reconnect with my better instincts. Like most of the important decisions in life, reversals like this come about when we allow ourselves to follow our heart lines—what really counts, what values you hold dear, what gifts you hope to offer—and notice all of the signs during the interview process, beyond the typical questions and business conversations, that indicate whether the organization you are about to join shares those qualities.

The day I announced my departure from Banana Republic, I remember the distraught faces of my team, whose confidence and devotion I had fought so hard to win. Many were proud to see me join a "true" luxury house, one where love of beauty, craft, and style might just trump any grid or chart they could divine. Others were angry that I jumped ship so quickly. I felt regretful, having started something I couldn't finish, abandoning those who cared enough to support my short-lived efforts, but my heart and soul were pointing elsewhere.

Why did Chanel finally hire me? I'll never know what was discussed behind closed doors, but here are a few of the reasons I gathered over time. On the surface, I had the right résumé: I spoke French, understood the culture, and had both marketing and retail experience. I had a great track record in growing a business and a strong reputation for leading teams. But beyond those achievements (and labels!), Chanel identified qualities they believed more crucial to the integrity of the brand and its many devotees both inside and outside the house. I believed in the power of creativity to lead the business, was ready to let go temporarily of my former identity as a president, unlearn everything I once knew to move from "mass to class," and wait three years before actually assuming my title of CEO.

Why did I go to Chanel? Well, you could say that it just felt right. Just like my first tweed jacket . . . it *suited* me.

ELEVEN

Embracing Paradox

I stood beneath the chandelier in Coco Chanel's apartment, neck craned, eyes wide open, as I soaked in the radiance of the amethyst and amber rock crystals, slender teardrops and swollen pear-shapes, that shimmered and twinkled above me. If you looked closely, my guide pointed out, you could spy the interlocking double Cs (just like Chanel's logo), Gs, (for Gabrielle, Chanel's birth name), and the number 5 (her lucky number and the name of her now-famous perfume) that had been braided into the wrought-iron branches of the fixture.

The guide tried to nudge me onward so we could visit the rest of the apartment's wonders, but I couldn't move. I was in awe. Every artifact I had seen, every anecdote I'd heard about this astonishing woman, was an object lesson in how originality, beauty, and style defy easy categorization and ready-made labels. Coco Chanel seemed to break every rule by combining seemingly opposite elements and by elegantly subverting convention to create something breathtakingly timeless and fresh. Even her ornately decorated apartment stood in stark contrast to her pared-down clothing designs. It was as if I were peeking into the soul of a true artist, a woman who refused to blindly accept the aesthetics of her time in order to invent her own. She represented everything I believed in and yearned to express.

A few days later, I watched as artisans in crisply ironed white coats delicately placed a nearly invisible film over the top of each N°5 perfume bottle and then tied black cotton cord around the neck. Each craftsman twirled the heated end of a wax stick around and around the dark thread in a perfect circle, then embossed it with double Cs. The process was repeated twice to ensure the best imprint of the tiny logo. Each and every bottle of this renowned fragrance was finished by hand to guarantee the utmost quality of its precious ingredients. It took exceptionally skilled workers to implement this intricate task, a technique called *baudruchage* dating back to the seventeenth century, which prevents air and water from diluting the purity of this iconic fragrance. Most companies had long abandoned the hand-sealing practice, but not Chanel. It preserved this time-honored tradition, a nod to the unique heritage of its creations.

Next I visited the distribution center, an enormous, nondescript bunker that had me convinced we'd arrived at the wrong address. High-tech robotics powered an assembly line of dollies stacked with cartons that whizzed by on gleaming silver tracks. Only a few humans were in sight amid the rows of floor-to-ceiling shelves piled high with boxes ready to ship. This, too, was Chanel, the very same company whose artisans embroidered intricate tweeds by hand, tailored each suit to the liking of each individual customer, and crafted one-of-a-kind pieces of jewelry. One foot in the future and one in the past, the House of Chanel was a study in contrasts.

At my first fashion show, in a seventeenth-century convent, I sat a few rows back, sandwiched between Chanel's discreet owners and other employees, as otherworldly models in intricately woven tweeds with handmade, jeweled buttons dotting the slim-fitted jackets ambled through the arcaded courtyard. I loved the elegant slit sleeves of those jackets, the frayed edges of the skirts, which added a new twist to Coco Chanel's classic designs. Many of the models' hands were slung in their pockets or rested on the top of their belts, giving the otherwise expensive collection a casual air. I marveled at the designer Karl Lagerfeld's seriousness and playfulness. He had an innate sense of how to reinvent Coco's design language with new shapes, materials, and trim. The possibilities seemed endless.

Back in New York, after a full year in Paris, I had begun to make myself comfortable in my new office. It was impossible to ignore the commanding views of Central Park, a riot of color this autumn, or to overlook the handles of the glass doors in the entry hall, shaped like the tops of the N°5 bottle. The large windows from my exquisitely decorated office made me feel as if I were actually living in a *tableau vivant*, floating with the drifting clouds. As I embarked on the next stage of my time at Chanel, I realized it would require me to hold *tout et son contraire en même temps* ("everything and its opposite at the same time"). That had been what Coco Chanel had done and what had made the brand an unparalleled success over the past century. Through my immersion in Chanel's history, I'd come to appreciate why that sensibility was so vital to the company and how difficult it was to maintain. The question was how I would be able to contribute to that legacy, embracing the paradox at the heart of the house's sustained success while also confronting pressing business challenges: one foot planted in the past, the other dipping its toe into the future.

◈

Shortly after joining the company, I was invited to the Met Ball, held by the Costume Institute at the Metropolitan Museum of Art. Like my dad, I tended to hug the wall at large gatherings, and I still felt awkward meeting new people, especially when they were larger-than-life characters like artists, celebrities, and rock stars—all of whom would be making their way to the Met Gala, too. (I still stung from the mortifying memory of my freshman year at Yale when I'd gushed to classmate Jodie Foster that she was my favorite actor, only to have her mumble thanks and hurry away.)

Tonight would be my first appearance at this celebrated gala. I was excited . . . and more than a little nervous. I was "hosting" a table. "Hosting" because the fashion and beauty brands pay large sums of money—at the time around $50,000 (now closer to $200,000—this ball does not seem to follow the national inflationary curve) to adorn their ten-to-twelve-seaters with the year's hippest, most beautiful, smartest, sexiest, and just most fabulous stars. What's more, Chanel was the subject of this year's Costume Institute's fashion exhibit. "Not a retrospective," Karl reminded

us. It was just two days before the auspicious May 5, 2005—
all 5s, which was Coco's favorite number and the day we were
also launching Baz Luhrmann's lush and romantic N°5 "film,"
the first three-minute ad to air on national TV, starring the in-
imitable Nicole Kidman. Neither Karl, Baz, nor Nicole would be
seated at my table, however. Their seats were smack dab in the
middle of the dining room, next to the Queen of the Ball herself,
Anna Wintour. The table I was hosting? It was in the nosebleed
section of the great Temple of Dendur—shabby by no means, but
hardly the center of the action. No matter. The Met Gala was de
rigueur, so despite my shyness and out-and-out fear of losing my
glass slipper before the bell struck midnight, I would go, make-
believing that I belonged in this world.

First, there was hair and makeup. I could hear the hairdresser
outside my office door chatting noisily with my assistant, waiting
his turn to transform this Cinderella into a princess. The last
time I had makeup was probably my high school prom. I remember scrubbing my face for hours to get the waterproof mascara off
to avoid looking like a depressed owl in the morning.

"I don't usually use foundation," I not-so-gently hinted to the
makeup artist, who seemed to be intent on creating some kind
of chef d'oeuvre from my just over forty-year-old face. I immediately regretted my bold statement. "I mean, I never really needed
much makeup at Old Navy. I've always worn the natural look."

"You have such beautiful skin; I'm just going to seal the
makeup with a little powder." *A little powder?* The makeup artist
dipped his brush for the seventh time into the pink fairy dust. "I

am going really light on you; you don't need much at all." *Really light?* I felt like I was being prepared for an appearance at the court of Louis XIV. I didn't dare turn my head too quickly, lest the façade crack and my impeccable mask fall off.

Next a hairdresser trooped into my office. When the PR team had arranged his visit, it had struck me as odd. What with my boy-cut style, I'd never required more than a fresh shampooing and a quick blow-dry, bypassing a brush entirely. Never mind, I wanted to look the part, so I deep-belly breathed to calm my nerves as the hairdresser ran his fingers through my lifeless mane. I had a flashback to a photo taken of me as a preteen back in Saint Louis, stringy hair framing my face. "Close your eyes, please." Clouds of aerosol spray made me cough, as the hairdresser's arms and hands swooped around my head.

And now, the dress. Or should I say, the *gown*. Antoine waited in the chair outside my office, busily tapping away on his Black-Berry. When he looked up, I noted surprise in his face. "Wow! You look really great." It was quite a contrast to my usual look: a pair of jeans, a black V-neck sweater, and Converse sneak-ers. The dress was long and black. Yes, just long and black. No adornment, no bells or whistles. I had rifled through pages of past couture collection catalogs to find something close to my pared-down aesthetic and settled on an elegant, strapless, floor-length sheath. Its only distinguishing feature was a deep V-neck, the deliciously glossy charmeuse fabric, and a long train. The cou-ture team had convinced me that since I was unwilling to bedeck myself in glittery details, the train was essential, even though I kept forgetting that it was actually attached to the dress (and thus to me) as I maneuvered from my desk to the outer office.

Naturally, it was raining that night, the windshield wipers keeping time as our black SUV idled in a long queue of traffic. We had left the office with only a few minutes' delay—I had been fussing with my strapless bra to be sure it would hold me through the night—and now I worried about missing the arrival time slot allotted to us. *What happens when you come late?* I wondered. *Do they still let you in or do you pay some kind of fine?* I looked from the invitation to the neon car clock and nervously counted the number of cars ahead of ours. If the dinner was at eight p.m., why did my invitation say six fifteen p.m.? I suspected that the uncool people were invited early to make room for the real celebs later. I was wrong.

"Jennifer, Jennifer, over here!" "Sarah, you look beautiful! Just one shot! Here!" "Salma, amazing dress! Love your look. Over here." "Renée, on your left, up here!" "Mick, Mick, slow down. We need a picture of you two. L'Wren, whose dress are you wearing?"

The raucous shouts and the incessant clicks of digital cameras drowned out the rain's pitter-patter as I stared into the flashing lights, half-expecting someone to call my name. I soon realized that no one was remotely interested in me. The paparazzi, cordoned off by thick velvet ropes, lined the edges of the steep red steps, alert and ready to strike should someone noteworthy come along. I quickly set my gaze downward, embarrassed that as we passed, the noisy bunch became silent. "Slow down," I whispered into Antoine's ear, holding on to his arm for dear life as we ascended the perilous stairs. The balls of my feet already ached, and my balance felt uncertain atop the six-inch heels. I began to worry whether my toes would survive being pinched into the neat pointy shoes.

Realizing that I would not be photographed, I began to relax and allowed myself to check out the stunning people around me as we continued to climb the stairs, that gorgeous train of fabric now arrayed picturesquely behind me. At about the halfway mark, I felt a slight tugging on the train, but not wanting to linger or be taken for some kind of celebrity stalker, I wrested the fabric free from the heel of my own shoe with a hasty jerk of my wrist. It was only when we reached the top of those interminable stairs that I realized I had torn a giant hole in the infamous train. I could feel my ears turn even redder; they were already a deep shade of scarlet, being pinched by the borrowed clip-on earrings—the very ones Nicole Kidman had worn in Baz's film.

By the time we reached the receiving line, I was a mess. Completely distraught by my ruined dress and unnerved by the noise and lights, I now would have to greet Anna, Karl, Nicole, and Baz, all members of the welcoming committee. I don't remember much of what happened next, only that when I leaned in to kiss Anna—I thought we were friends by then, having had a one-on-one lunch at the Four Seasons—she offered me her hand to shake instead. I made my way into the immense hall for cocktails, looking through the marble arches to find the nearest wall to keep me company.

Miraculously the rest of the evening went without a hitch. The sight of so many spectacular gowns and elegant tuxes threw enough stardust into my eyes to help me forget the torn train and that little gaffe with Anna Wintour. I even had my own brush with stardom when one of my idols, Mick Jagger, gallantly touched my waist, sidestepping me on the stairs as he and his girlfriend, fashion designer L'Wren Scott, were ascending. It was impossible not to be seduced by this new world filled with celebrities, luxury, and glamour. I could understand why some end up lost, chasing each new hot trend and schmoozing with the latest hipsters. I could see why so many of my colleagues might forget their own last names in favor of whatever luxury brand employed them. But that hadn't been the way Coco Chanel had made her mark (even if she did befriend many artists and socialites), and I realized it wouldn't be the way I'd make mine at Chanel. I may not have found my footing quite yet, but I knew I would, and I wouldn't be wearing six-inch heels.

❖

The distant whirr of traffic fell silent when the heavy wood door shut behind us as we entered the Gothic castle atop a hill off Sunset Boulevard. A rush of anticipation flowed through my veins, and my heart skipped a beat, as I remembered all of the photographs I had seen and stories I had read about the famous people who had inhabited these well-guarded interiors. Wild parties, elegant weddings, passionate love trysts, scandalous spats, police raids, drug busts, suicides—the Chateau Marmont was a

Hollywood icon and still fashionable with the coolest celebrities and industry insiders, some of whom had plopped down on over-stuffed couches in its musty lounge, a few stragglers having a late breakfast on this sunny afternoon. I headed to the elevators, accompanied by the director of Chanel's creative team. We spoke in hushed whispers and treaded lightly down the cavernous hallway to a luxury suite. We were here to meet a star and to convince her to become the *égérie* (muse) of our Coco Mademoiselle fragrance campaign. My choice wasn't the obvious one; in fact, she was barely known at the time and not even nineteen years old—a far cry from our last spokesmodel, Kate Moss, who was one of the most recognizable faces and highest-paid models in the industry. It was risky and pushed the bounds of what some of our most loyal customers and dedicated employees might have considered "on brand." What's more, I had already convinced the powers that be to accept another, more established actress, and now I was reversing course. But my instincts were pulling me toward taking a chance on this bright, new talent.

Tall, slender, with warm, brown eyes and impossibly high cheekbones, she greeted us with a smile. "Hi, I'm Keira. It's lovely to meet you. Lindy [her agent] has told me so much about you."

I noticed how clear and fresh Keira Knightley's complexion was, even without a hint of makeup. So elegant, yet so completely at ease, she walked ahead of us dressed in torn jeans and a roomy sweatshirt. "Lindy and Mum are out on the terrace. Just have a seat while I get some fresh iced tea."

I had seen *Bend It Like Beckham* several years prior and remembered making a mental note of the actor who played Jules, a
spunky young female "footballer" determined to pursue her sport
despite her mother's often-sexist objections. In the film, Jules
"bends the ball" and the rules, denying her mother the pleasure
of seeing her daughter clad in frilly skirts and floral tops, opting
instead for her "trackies" and sneakers. Rather than search for
a boyfriend, Jules devotes her time to practice and to sponsoring her best friend, an Indian girl forbidden to play the sport
by her conservative parents. Keira's allure in that role, uncom-
mon for a young starlet, reminded me of Jean Seberg in Godard's
Breathless—her liveliness and overtly boyish charm enhancing
her seductiveness and sensuality. Her athletic build, shagged
and streaked bob, and puckish smile suggested self-assurance,
an inner confidence. She would do things her way even if the
world had something else in mind. Her fierceness and determination, paired with tenderness and vulnerability, reminded me of
the young Gabrielle Chanel working her way from seamstress to
Paris's doyenne of fashion. Jules was Keira's first major role, and
it told me everything about who she might be.

I had been riveted by the stories of Chanel's spare beginnings,
her rise to fame, and her loss of true love. Born near the turn of
the century, an orphan becomes the queen of the fashion world,
seduces men and women alike, is influenced by artists and, in
turn, inspires them, and then works until the day she dies. I
remembered viewing a series of famous photos of Coco Chanel
during my training period in Paris. In one, her strong and seduc-

tive regard as she glances over her shoulder, cigarette in hand, pearls sensually draped down her back, captures all of her inherent contradictions. In another, she sits atop a horse, radiating athleticism in simple trousers, a white shirt, and soft black tie. And there she is in a white dress, firm, tanned arms poised on the dinner table as she entertains her artist friends at a ball in Monte Carlo. How relaxed and modern she looks at the beach, with her newsboy cap and aviators, gazing off into the distance, observing the world around her. How elegant and self-assured, one arm draped on the mantel above a fireplace as she poses in the very first ad for her singular fragrance, N°5. How at ease she appears in her *marinière* (blue-and-white-striped sailor's shirt) near a field of wildflowers, hands casually in her pockets. How focused her gaze when the camera catches her image refracted over and over in the faceted mirror on the stairs of the rue Cambon. Sophisticated and rustic, refined and athletic, joyous and sad, arduous and playful—she embraced paradox in everything she did.

I was fascinated by this legend, but even more enthralled by who Chanel came to be and the legacy she left for women around the world. Chanel was more than a designer; she was a symbol and an archetype for strong women. And her life was more than just personal history; it was a meta-story of femininity, embodying all of the complexities of today's woman: masculine/feminine, driven/sensitive, determined/alluring. Chanel refused to act like other women who sat idly at home, waiting on their spouses while playing parlor games with friends. She rejected the constricting and overly decorated clothing of her times, as well as the sickly sweet, floral perfumes. She wanted to work, to create, and to produce clothes that would allow women all of the same comforts men enjoyed and to invent a fragrance "that smelled like a woman." Her designs, now seemingly so simple, so classic, were nothing short of revolutionary at the time. She bucked all of the constraints of her era, eliminated the corsets, high necklines, and floor-length skirts that inhibited a woman's natural breath and movement. Stealing menswear fabrics to shape them into feminine silhouettes, she created a whole new vernacular for design and a new way for women to exist in the world, one that was neither masculine nor feminine but *both* at the same time. And she created a scent, Chanel N°5, which for the first time combined aldehydes and natural flowers, smelling unlike anything before it. I admired her resolve and resilience, but I was even more enchanted by how completely she subverted everything she touched.

Something told me that Keira Knightley was a modern-day version of Chanel. Both women defined who they wanted to be beyond any convention or label: Chanel, by introducing a wholly new way for women to dress and therefore exist in a restrictive society, and Keira, by rejecting the ingénue roles typical of Hollywood starlets in favor of playing a tomboy in her debut film. Two different eras. Two different domains. Each woman demonstrated her own kind of self-possession and commitment to the strength and power of her full femininity.

"I'm not much of a fashionista." Keira pointed apologetically to her ripped jeans and sweatshirt. "I mean, I love clothes but I don't know, I've just never really been into that scene, you know?" She tilted her head with a gamine grin, her eyebrows arching upward just a little mischievously.

I knew that my role wasn't so much to sell Keira as it was to invite her to participate in a legend. She had read a little about Coco Chanel and was intrigued by her story. Besides, Keira said, "Mum showed me those gorgeous ads with Catherine Deneuve. So classy."

Perfect, I thought. "We have this fragrance, Coco Mademoiselle—it represents who Chanel was when she was a young woman and coming into her own."

Keira beamed. "Oh, I like that fragrance. Mum, isn't that the one you bought me?" Her mom nodded encouragingly.

"It's meant to capture the essence and spirit of this brave, independent young woman, who through her energy, determination, confidence, and desire crafted her own destiny," I said. "I saw you in *Bend It Like Beckham* and immediately felt like you could really incarnate that woman. Just like Jules in the movie, Chanel created her own path."

Keira's eyes brighten while I continued. "As you probably know, Chanel's mother died when she was young, and her father abandoned her at an orphanage in Aubazine, the center of France." I turned to include Lindy and Keira's mother because I could feel their interest coming alive as well. "She learned how to sew, then found work as a seamstress, while at night she sang in the local cabarets."

Keira was enraptured. By the time I finished the story, we had added a new member to our Chanel family. The collaboration with Keira was a wild success. The perfume, Coco Mademoiselle, quickly grew to take on top market share around the world.

❖

Another year later, I found myself hosting a table of a different kind, this time not at the Met but in Neuilly just outside of Paris, home to Chanel's global headquarters. It wasn't a fancy party or an unfamiliar setting. It didn't require a ball gown or contrived social graces. I was now at the *head* of a conference room table in meetings where I had previously only been a participant— finally the global CEO, the boss. After running the US business, where I worked with local teams to upgrade the brand's presence, create a clear vision, and build alliances with my partners in France, I was now set to lead the global executive team of ten men, all dressed in some variation of tailored blue and gray suits, tasteful CC-laden ties, and spit-shiny shoes. Poised at the edge of my chair, my back slightly arched to make myself feel taller, I reached to tug down my American Apparel tank top to be sure it covered the top of my J Brand jeans. With much inspiration from Chanel I had created my own uniform, mixing casual with dressy—a Chanel jacket and denim. But that's not the only paradox I would need to embrace.

Minutes passed while I waited for everyone to get coffee, finish off the oven-fresh *croissants au chocolat*, and quiet down for some serious business. I looked around room. The air felt thick with the discomfort of uncertainty. During this meeting, like so many others, we would need to discuss important but controversial initiatives to implement as we grew and adapted to the interconnected, global world. Because of Chanel's rich history, any change, however small, was never easy and required thorough consideration. We would work through a series of strategic decisions, often contentious in nature, which required support and approval from every person on the team (each of whom ran a different business unit, geographical region, or function), and subsequently, everyone else on their teams. By now, I had *mostly* conquered any awkward feelings of inadequacy I'd experienced in my first years with the company. Agenda in hand, I was ready to assume my full responsibilities.

I say *mostly* because the task at hand was daunting. By 2007, Chanel was already on the ascent to becoming a mega-brand. New economies like China were just beginning to fill the luxury bubble with hot air; customer demand for our products was surging. With more than eighty years of history, undeniably exquisite creations, and impeccable images, Chanel pulled out ahead of most of the competition, cementing its already immutable iconic status. Stepping in as CEO of an already successful business, a brand larger than life, with a team of experienced, seasoned leaders was intimidating, to say the least. How would I lead this team into the future? How would I define myself as a CEO? Inspired again by our founder, I began to consider how I might subvert the label and redefine it.

First, given the uncertain world we were entering, I decided that commanding the troops would no longer work. My leadership wouldn't be about espousing some grandiose vision and waving the flag for all to follow. Instead, I needed to ask questions, lots of questions, and inspire others to do the same. I had noticed during my training period, when I was asked not to voice an opinion, how beneficial asking a series of naïve but pointed questions was both to me and to those I questioned. I could listen for what tensions and concerns lay just under the surface. I could mine the nuggets of truth and sort through what people really cared about, spotting what might be tired assumptions and untested biases. I decided to approach all meetings innocently, asking a dozen "why" questions and just as many "why not's." What might have looked like naïveté at first glance became a form of wisdom. By asking particularly gnarly questions—even questions others were too afraid to ask—I stimulated entirely new conversations and demonstrated that it was acceptable, even safe, to *not know* all of the answers. Eventually, this type of salient curiosity became contagious; other members of the team also started asking more deliberate questions, and we all became engaged, collectively, in creating Chanel's future.

Most executives obsess about the competition. Rather than comparing ourselves to competitors and following their lead, I asked the teams to focus on what *we* did well, what we were known for (something I heard Mickey say more than a thousand times), what set us apart from all of the other brands, and how we might polish the apple. How could we bring Chanel forward in all of its most astonishing magnificence, from our rich history to our radical modernity? The same was true for my executive team. Rather than lob criticisms at one another or sift through presentations for errors—which is one of the ways savvy executives often try to prove their worth and smarts to each other—I asked that we listen to each other's comments for what was interesting. Finding something compelling in someone's thoughts rather than calling out all of the reasons why they weren't perfectly right helped us reimagine our business. Frequently it was the least vocal or most offbeat person who presented some of the more thought-provoking insights. Instead of shutting them down, I pointed out their relevance.

Homing in on our strengths didn't mean we could ignore evaluating and rethinking our business. On the contrary, we would have to listen much more to our customers, our employees, and the world around us. However, unlike many CEOs who spend time mired in consumer research and financial results, I realized it was equally critical to step back from the operational details of day-to-day responsibilities to see bigger trends and movements outside our industry. I revised the format of all of our regular meetings to make them less systematic and rote, adding offsite events and outside speakers to broaden our view and to provoke us to test our assumptions. I encouraged teams to bring works in progress, rather than fully baked presentations, to the table so that we could all bat around our future opportunities and risks. I added new members to the executive team to bring in more strategic thinking and offer new angles on the business, and eventually I balanced the group by adding six women. Career development usually means grooming successors within their areas of expertise. Taking a riskier approach, I encouraged and supported key talent to move into jobs where they had little or no experience but rather a certain capacity or affinity. These less obvious placements strengthened the brand by offering out-of-the-box perspectives, but it also allowed employees to develop new skills and to discover where their true talents may lie. Even for those on the executive team already solidly anchored in their positions, I spent much of my time providing them with one-on-one mentoring, not just giving them course-correcting feedback, as many boss/employee sessions normally go, but encouraging them to alloy their talents and passions with a sense of purpose.

I didn't realize it at first, but I was working my way toward a form of leadership considerably different from the one typically handed down from one CEO to the next. I took the title of CEO, but I didn't accept the usual labels that attach themselves to that position. My inspirations came from remarkable women like Coco Chanel but also from mavericks like Mickey Drexler; from the mind-blowing idea of deconstructionism and New Wave cinema; from Fleur's daring pragmatism; from Dizzy Gillespie's rule-bending riffs; from the journey I'd made from "mass to class" as I left The Gap for Chanel. It was, indeed, a matter of embracing paradoxes.

◈

I realized that the form of leadership I was practicing might just help all of us to confront the increasing complexities of our business climate. We would all need to embrace paradox and subvert our past ways of leading in order to thrive in such rapidly and dramatically changing times. I didn't want to rely on outside consultants touting their own "leadership models" or frameworks, and I also didn't want to prescribe or enforce a set of "competencies" or "leadership qualities" that had been printed on fancy typeset cards and distributed to all employees, only to gather dust in the bottom drawer of someone's desk. I had seen enough mission statements turn to fossilized, sterile diktats, and I yearned to explore and bring forward my own authenticity and invite the same in the team. This journey needed to be personal for me as well as for others. The answers didn't lie in textbooks but rather in the individuals themselves.

With encouragement and a renewed commitment from my executive team, and a collaborative design process, we launched an initiative we called the Active and Conscious Leadership Journey. The paradoxical combination of the words "Active" and "Conscious" were meant to reinforce the internal *and* external focus we needed. Internal because good leaders are self-aware; they work to continually improve themselves and expand their own capabilities. They know and benefit from their strengths just as they recognize and watch their shadow sides. They know what motivates and excites them and what triggers them, so they manage themselves just as they manage others. External, because good leaders are always in the "act" of leading. They listen as much to others as they listen to themselves. They know their own business segment and they are also attuned to the world at large.

They are inquisitive and have an insatiable curiosity that leads them past well-worn paths and patterns.

We decided to call it a "journey" rather than a program because it wasn't meant to be a onetime event but an ongoing process. The work was something we would all experience together and use collectively to improve relationships. We would work from the "inner"—looking introspectively at ourselves as leaders—to the "outer"—how we connect to each other, our teams, our business, and the world at large.

As such, the top twenty executives and I spent a full year in this learning process before eventually expanding it to hundreds of our global leaders around the world. Each leader selected a personal coach and a quality that he or she hoped to improve or enhance. I decided to mentor everyone; touching base frequently, we discussed their wins and frustrations, their successes and struggles. Over the course of a year, we invited a series of outside speakers—from the poet David Whyte to peace builder Scilla Elworthy to management guru Dan Pink to top business strategist Clay Christensen—to share their insights and then work alongside us over the course of several sessions to tackle our specific challenges. (In the following years, we included others, including Caroline McHugh, author and "IDologist," and Hal Gregersen, co-author of *The Innovator's DNA* with Jeffrey Dyer and Clay Christensen and executive director at the MIT Leadership Center.) It was during this time that several top executives accompanied me to the ranch in California for some horse whispering.

The results of that year's leadership journey as well as the two years that followed were a breakthrough, thanks to the unwavering devotion of Chanel's executive teams and the many coaches and speakers who supported them. Business units banded together to launch innovative projects, teams implemented new business approaches for age-old issues, and we began to explore the brand's deeper purpose. What moved me the most were the hundreds of letters of gratitude I received after these sessions. Some described how the journey had helped them personally and professionally. They mentioned being more open to new ideas, listening more carefully to others, letting go of assumptions, and observing the world with fresh eyes. Some talked about a renewed sense of purpose in their jobs and at home. Naturally, some expressed frustration; they'd hope to see bigger, better, and faster results. I reminded them that, like all journeys, this one would take time, patience, and persistence.

I am proud to have left this legacy at Chanel as the work has now touched countless people and continues in my absence. It represents a new horizon of possibilities—for leaders and for the world. When we are able to open our ears and our minds, more innovative ideas will emerge. When we work beyond labels to embrace people with different perspectives, everyone benefits. When we're able to let go of preconceived notions, our truest selves come into focus.

❖

Creativity so often stems from paradoxes—pairing two seemingly opposing ideas, qualities, designs, or objects to invent something surprising, unexpected, and ultimately desirable. It's these unpredictable combinations that make some personalities so irresistible and products so coveted. They don't fit the mold. They don't quite follow the rules—they bend them to make something new. I once read a quote by E. E. Cummings that said, "The Artist is no other than he who unlearns what he has learned, in order to know himself." The process he describes is the continual subversion of what you know or what exists to get closer to who you are—a form of going beyond any given label. It's not always easy to pursue this type of paradox, to push against a system or set of beliefs that have defined you in the past, or even to challenge the definition of the role you find yourself in now. But embracing your own paradoxes or, as Cummings says, unlearning enough of what you have learned to know more about yourself, allows you to develop a far more compelling perspective and, ultimately, contribution.

Are you doing enough to stimulate your curiosity? What would it mean to be the artist of your own life? In other words, how have you challenged the status quo to invent something new? What have you unlearned lately to better know yourself? I have tried to become the artist of my life by continually questioning what has existed, jumping into unfamiliar situations, absorbing new contexts, and, eventually, finding a different way to be. Are you willing to ask these kinds of questions of yourself and others and, alternatively, can you play by the rules and bend them to make yourself distinctive?

TWELVE

Cutting the Corset

A diminutive woman stepped up to the podium; she was wearing a cream-colored silk jacket sprinkled with winding vines and pink blossoms, an elegant green skirt, and tiny gold earrings, and her hair was adorned with fresh roses.

I had never heard her speak but I already knew about her efforts and, like many, I had admired her steady, nonviolent determination to eliminate corruption and bring democracy to Burma. Here was a woman who had been confined under house arrest for fifteen years as a result of her tireless fight for human rights and democracy in her country, a feat for which she had been awarded the Nobel Peace Prize in 1991. A person who refused to succumb to violence as a means to an end. A leader who, against all odds, influenced the militaristic regime and obtained a minority position for her party in Burma's parliament.

Her delicate frame belied what a powerful force Aung San Suu Kyi has become around the world. After her release from house arrest, Daw Suu, as she is known, chose to work with the very same military leaders who had imprisoned her because she believed diplomacy would further her cause for democracy. When she received the Congressional Gold Medal, she was allowed to bring only one person to the ceremony; she chose the highest-ranking military officer in the country to accompany her, knowing the good press it would create for him. Daw Suu makes a point to speak often about how much respect she has for the military and her desire to work with them. Her actions have decreased the fear that they have toward her, even convincing these same people, those who had tried to diminish her presence, that it would be in their interest to give her a voice.

In her story, there is humanity. She joked about her past, how she "broke the law" when attending Oxford University by riding her bike the wrong way down a one-way street. When asked about what she might have done differently if she had known she would be under house arrest for so long, she revealed that she wished she'd practiced the piano more as a child and given her teacher less of a hard time. "It would have given me much solace throughout the years," she told us. She showed up as herself. She laughed at herself. She revealed her own vulnerabilities without apology or shame.

And it wasn't just her words; I was equally intrigued by what she wore and how she held herself. You might expect her to be hardened and tough. But Daw Suu stood before us with those beautiful red roses in her hair, her signature look, and a wonderfully feminine outfit. Despite her fierce resolve and her personal sacrifice, Daw Suu wasn't afraid to express femininity. Being a woman was not a handicap but an advantage, a source of strength.

Other accounts of her leadership underscore these qualities.

When she faced the military during a peaceful university rally, college-age soldiers stared down college students through the crosshairs of their rifles, both parties visibly frightened. Daw Suu stood up in the crowd and gently put her hand on the end of the commanding officer's rifle, firmly pointing the weapon toward the ground. With this one gesture, the military backed away from the students. By acknowledging the common humanity of these opposing groups, she used empathy to prevent harm and destruction.

In these moments and many others, her strength lay in embracing the very same feminine qualities that others may have called soft, conciliatory, or weak. Daw Suu embodied a different kind of power, one coming from an enduring, internal sense of what she valued and her purpose in life. This extraordinary empathy was beyond anything I had experienced. And to believe so fundamentally in your cause that you would be willing to sacrifice your own needs and desires—her commitment was beyond anything I had known.

Although my circumstances were far less dramatic, I couldn't help considering how my own femininity had also been the single biggest source of my strength. I thought back to my early days on the road for L'Oréal and how putting myself in the shoes of Mr. Dupont, the hypermarket buyer, had allowed me to speak his language, grasp what he cared about, and provide both of us with a common solution. Later, after Mickey taught me to listen (especially when I felt absolutely sure of my point), I noticed how opening my perspective allowed for more innovative alternatives in our business decisions. I remembered times like the one in Hong Kong with Damon when I needed to stand by my convictions, calmly but resolutely, regardless of the consequences. Throughout my career, I had worked to listen to, to understand, and even to integrate the opinions of less collaborative colleagues, including those opponents who actively tried to stymie my efforts. I'd been open to their perspectives, but I'd also tried to be true to my own.

I reflected on some of the other women in my life who'd inspired me: Catherine (in *Jules and Jim*), my teacher Ms. Moceri, Fleur, Coco Chanel, Keira Knightley, and other strong figures whose purpose or uncompromising art I admired from afar, including Gloria Steinem, Simone de Beauvoir, Toni Morrison, Virginia Woolf, Nina Simone, Madonna, Lady Gaga, Yayoi Kusama, and Cindy Sherman. They all refused to shy away from a certain quality of femininity or from redefining the very notion of femininity itself by incarnating their own version. All had a keen sense of who they were and what they hoped to achieve. All braved some resistance for challenging societal norms. Whatever our talents and our ambitions, we can all learn from women who cut loose from expectations.

✛

After hearing Aung San Suu Kyi share her story, I decided to investigate this notion of feminine leadership more deeply. Research on the subject tends to characterize feminine leadership with labels such as self-awareness, empathy, vulnerability, curiosity, and agility, whereas archetypal masculine leadership tends to be defined by decisiveness, confidence, focus, and strategy.

This second list of traits is what companies have traditionally expected their leaders to cultivate in themselves and in others. And with good reason. Can you imagine a company run by a leader or group of leaders without focus, strategy, determination, and decisiveness?

Still, the more I considered the assumptions and associations of each of these poles, the more I could see how women and men alike have been trapped by these narrow formulations and often err on the side of adopting behaviors endorsed by society—notably those labeled "masculine." I understand how it happens, of course. We tend to model the behavior and the attitudes we've seen before; we imitate and we posture to fit someone else's definition of success. It may seem like it's working, at least for a time, but too often we find ourselves constricted and conflicted—disconnected from our values and our purpose. Even then, we continue to play these roles because that's the way the game has always been played; that's the way leaders get evaluated and rewarded—that's the way to win. Or is it?

Although "feminine" qualities are sometimes mentioned and even lauded, they usually take a backseat to these more concrete and result-driven "masculine" traits. We rarely recognize the power and effectiveness of what so many companies define as "nice to haves." As a result, both men and women learn to minimize qualities that don't conform to the conventional model of leadership—putting aside those so-called feminine leadership traits.

But I was now seeing that "the top" was in dire need of more feminine strengths to navigate such an infinitely complex world. While masculine, command-and-control models may have worked in the industrial age, this one-sided approach to leadership no longer suits the ambiguous environment in which most leaders and their organizations operate. With rapid change comes uncertainty and, yes, paradox. That's why the qualities of curiosity—of asking, not telling—and agility need to be cultivated and encouraged in leaders of every persuasion.

I started to understand that if women weren't rising to the top more often, it wasn't only because they weren't "leaning in" or weren't just as ambitious as their male counterparts. It wasn't just because corporate policies didn't allow enough time for maternity leave or the flextime needed to raise families. These things were, and still are, crucial and must be addressed. But the underlying issue, the nut no one had cracked, was what *kind* of leadership we value and how we teach, assess, and promote "good" leaders in all organizations—whether women or men. Until more feminine qualities take an equal place in our companies, until leaders are required to demonstrate the equally crucial skills that many women inherently possess and draw upon every day, until we go beyond worn-out labels, even these important changes in policy won't have lasting impact.

I want *us* to change the frame of leadership itself—to consider more broadly all of the qualities we might need to navigate such increasing complexity—but also represent the inherent beauty and power of femininity that had always been so important to my own life as it has in so many others'.

It's not so easy to be a woman climbing to the top. I know what it's like to have your legs gain more respect than your hard work and how emotionally draining it is to get on a plane to Hong Kong six weeks after giving birth. I know how unusual I am to have even had these challenges to confront. I'm still one of the paltry 4 percent of women who have actually risen to the role of CEO. As a result, I feel a responsibility to try to create change so that more women and *more men* can succeed by being who they are. The responsibility for change rests with all of us. By moving beyond the label, we can *all* make our workplaces and our lives more effective and more equitable.

❖

"I don't stand here on behalf of any company or brand. I'm just here as myself. I am here as a woman, as a luxury customer, as a merchant, who once coveted the exquisite beauty of luxury from the outside, and as an executive, who's spent the better part of the last fifteen years learning and grappling with the actual business of luxury from the inside."

Those were some of my first lines from a speech I gave at the International Luxury Conference hosted by the *New York Times* in April 2016, just a few months after I bid farewell to Chanel. Saying good-bye to a brand, a team, and a business I loved was incredibly hard. It had been a wonderful ride, and I am eternally grateful for the opportunity to have shepherded Chanel into the new millennium.

Thanks to my earlier shopping expedition to Jeffrey, I had found the perfect post-Chanel outfit: a navy, form-fitting jersey dress with a scalloped-edge detail, designed by Azzedine Alaia, and a sheer periwinkle blouse to wear over it. My choices were intentional—the dress, not too loud or too "fashion-y," classic but chic, conservative but also sexy. I admired Alaia because he resists trends, always designing clothes that flatter the feminine silhouette, and showing his collections outside of the regularly scheduled industry calendar. (He doesn't participate in Paris Fashion Week.) Upon arriving at the venue, I'd had a good laugh with the *New York Times* fashion director and chief fashion critic, Vanessa Friedman, who'd invited me to speak. We'd both inadvertently chosen similar dresses by the same designer. Another fantastic thing about Alaia's designs? To paraphrase one of Gabrielle Chanel's famous aphorisms, they show the woman wearing the dress, not the other way around.

Just to be sure I looked svelte in my new dress with its clingy jersey material, I had also worn a pair of "control top" panties, a euphemism for a girdle. They definitely held me in, so much so that I could barely breathe as I rehearsed my speech for the umpteenth time on the way to the conference. About halfway through my rehearsal, right there in the car, I shimmied my way out of this fabric prison. Coco was right—corsets have no place on a woman's body.

I greeted the few people I knew as I broached the entryway and noticed a small cluster of well-dressed attendees glancing my direction with genuine curiosity; a few others trained their eyes across the room, avoiding my gaze. At the time, I wanted to believe they just didn't know who I was—after all, I had done only a few public appearances during my tenure at Chanel. I willfully ignored that my photograph had been on all of the invitations and advertising, not to mention that my departure from Chanel had made major industry news. I realized that no one quite knew what to say to me—just yet. Without an official title, I felt a bit like an act in the sideshow of a circus: odd, maybe interesting, certainly worthy of attention, but not so easy to categorize.

I hid out in the "green room" (a converted conference space), pacing as I ran the speech through my head one more time. I was going to expose and put in context what many already knew threatened the value and even existence of luxury—notably, the Internet, globalization, and the new customer and employee base who now demanded so much more than products from companies and brands alike. And I was, for the first time outside of a university talk, going to reveal my own journey and my discovery that a new form of leadership might just be at the heart of solving these impending threats.

Research shows that few people manage to keep their New Year's resolution, but setting an "intention" for the year can be a powerful way to set your course, achieve goals, and hitch your day-to-day actions to a higher purpose. In 2015, my last year as the CEO of Chanel, my word had been "Truth." I had been struggling to stay tethered to my own inner truth as competing opinions and priorities swirled around me. Whenever things got too hectic or confusing, I'd remind myself of that word—*truth*—and, like magic, I would start to feel like I was back on solid ground. I had to keep asking myself: Did I want to give my truth a face, or did I want to put a mask on it? It occurred to me that we all have our own inner truth. You can sponsor and help it emerge, or you can ignore it for a time, but eventually lack of sun will cause it to shrivel.

Truth doesn't exist without a voice. I chose "Voice" as my word for 2016. As much as I enjoyed dressing in tweeds and camellias, flying in first class, and getting reservations at fashionable restaurants, I needed to reclaim my authenticity. Remaining silent meant that my truth didn't fully exist. So many of us have a deeply felt sense of who we are and what we can best bring to the world, but we hold back in favor of "coloring in the lines" and playing by other people's rules. I have chosen to give voice to my truths and share them with others in hopes that they, too, can come forward with their own.

Now that I have "cut the corset," I am not exactly sure what my next adventure will be—whether I'll find myself once again at the helm of another luxury house, back in the throes of a crazy start-up, or seated at yet another boardroom table leading a venture I have yet to discover. But I do know this: I care deeply about creating beauty in the world. I care deeply about shifting the frames of reference so that both women and men can become leaders who are true to themselves. I care deeply about contributing in a positive way to our next generation.

As I approached the podium that day, I felt calm and composed, but I also felt entirely exposed—for the first time in a long time. I am always a little bit jumpy before giving a speech, but this time I was also exhilarated, the way one feels the moment before jumping into a swimming pool on a hot day. I stood onstage in silence for a noticeable pause, just taking in the audience and feeling my own sturdy legs beneath me. I could hear the sound of my own voice vibrate as I began to speak, the words shaped from a whole new place inside me. The ground felt solid. I wasn't reciting the company line, I wasn't trying to say something popular, and I wasn't trying to gain anyone's approval. I had found a voice of my own. I felt completely myself, unabashed for speaking my mind, proud to share my point of view. I had spoken from a place of truth, one unfiltered and unbiased by anyone else.

Committing to Truth and Voice also impacted my personal life. After being together for twenty-eight years, Antoine and I decided to evolve our relationship, again going beyond the label. We ended our marriage and started separate and different chapters of our lives, each opening ourselves to new love while continuing to cherish the bond we've had. Our love, in Antoine's words, is "transcendent, pushing the boundaries of what is possible." While we are no longer in the romantic form of our relationship, we will always be partners, best friends, and family.

I continue to practice using my voice and to encourage all those lit majors and film geeks, those shy and self-conscious trainees, those soul-searching executives, and especially professional women told to "ask like a man" to come forward with their own truths, to go beyond the label, and to lead their lives as only they can.

ACKNOWLEDGMENTS

A book doesn't ever get written alone, especially this one. My loved ones, friends, family, teachers, and colleagues in and beyond the stories of my life didn't just help me write this book, they *are* the book. They all gave parts of themselves to me, unselfishly and often selflessly. They are the true coauthors of this book and in so many ways, my life.

Thank you and deep gratitude:

To Antoine, my "was-band," my "ride or die" guy, and forever, "pupuce," whose contributions are way too large to list but whose endless commitment and support taught me the true meaning of unconditional love. Pauline and Camille "Mimi," my two most treasured creations who never cease to surprise me and make me infinitely proud. My mom, with whose belief I could do anything, and whose tender heart, nurturing love, and care, gave me the confidence to try things I might otherwise imagine well beyond my reach. My father, whose wise advice continues to astonish me and whose trust in me has allowed me to be at home in whatever label I might take on. My sisters, Suzanne and Andrea, who put up with me all those years and loved me even when I asked them to turn their music down lower than a whisper so I could study. To my wonderful teachers at John Burroughs High School—Ellen

Moceri, one of the first who piqued my interest in great literature by introducing me to Tolstoy and Dostoyevsky and showed me how a woman can be the boss. Kathy Stanley, to whom I owe, in part, my great love of France. And to the late John Faust whose obsession with theater was contagious and whose snarky jokes lightened my sometimes overly serious mood. To the Novis family and the Talamon family, who welcomed me with open arms into their lives and each in their own way opened my eyes to beauty. Colombe, my dear friend and longtime partner in crime who kept me laughing for so many years and showed me new ways to "get what you need." To my inspirational professors at Yale: Annette Insdorf, whose insights and observations on the great films of the New Wave never left me; Master T. who "embodied" his work better than anyone I've known; and Diane Kleiner, who taught me how to connect artifacts to create narratives. To Alain Styl, who demonstrated how to follow and bend the rules at the same time, and Philippe Sauter, who gave a young upstart the gift of his friendship and through whose eyes I learned to see beauty where others often could not. Agnes Visage for her good humor, heart, and confidence, who helped me navigate my first real job. To Dan Walker, for first identifying me as a "merchant" even though nothing on my résumé indicated it was so. Mark Smith and Peter Richter, my favorite "vendors," who took a shot on a naïve, inexperienced retail trainee and showed her the ropes. To Nancy Green, without whose trust and support I would probably have stayed in the sample closet and my good friend and mentor Jenny Ming, who demonstrated every day what it meant to be an effective and powerful leader without ever having to raise her voice. To Kerry Radcliffe, whose valuable counsel and partnership helped me become a better leader. To all of my other colleagues and friends at The Gap, Old Navy, and Banana Republic for teaching me everything I needed to know about American retail, making my fifteen years there some of the most exciting of my life. And of course, to Mickey: I couldn't have asked for a better guide, mentor, and friend. His insight and unflinching support during and after my Gap years have been invaluable. To Melanie Kusin and Tim Boerkel, who could see the chic in a mass-market Francophile. Floriane de St. Pierre for a rigorous but inspiring interview and, many years later, excellent collaboration. Alan Spizman for his kindness and palpable humanity. To the owners of Chanel for taking a chance on me, guiding and supporting me during my tenure at the house. My team, colleagues, and friends at Chanel, for their commitment and devotion to a novel and progressive leadership approach and especially to those who stood by, believed in, and supported me over my thirteen years there. To David Whyte, Scilla Elworthy, Clay Christensen, Hal Gregersen, and Caroline McHugh, whose wisdom, vision, and participation in the Active and Conscious Leadership Journey made my experiences and those of so many others richer and more fulfilling; and to all the coaches who supported and gave their love and time to this work. To Martha Beck and Koelle Simpson (and many horses), who taught me and so many others what owning your power and using your energy feels like. To the lovely Keira Knightley, whose spunk and grace continue to inspire me, and her wonderful agent, Lindy King, whose warmth and kindness made her a perfect ally. To Jeffrey Kalinsky and his team at the boutique, who styled me out of tweed jackets and into the latest fashions—and my newest identity. To Linda Lorimer and Julie Thibault, my dear friends, for their keen, on-point feedback on the manuscript and loving support for my voice. To Alfonso Nunez, Charlie Mullaly, and Brad Gilden for keeping my body, heart, and soul aligned after too many days bent over a keyboard. To my close friend Zainab Salbi, who has held my hand during my darkest hours over the past years and for whose light and love I am forever grateful. To Betsy Rapoport, brilliant editor and writing coach, who convinced me (despite my own self-critic) that I knew how to write, who wowed me with the first outline for a story I didn't know I had, and whose encouragement, gentle direction, and unwavering dedication kept me going even when I didn't think I could. To my agent, Jim Levine, for understanding the nuances of my book, helping me find the perfect publisher, and doing one of the best imitations of Terry Gross I've ever seen. His sharp observations gave more depth and meaning to everything I had to say. To the women at HarperCollins, whose enthusiasm, good style, and engagement in that first meeting had me before "hello," for believing and investing in me and this book. To my extraordinary editor and beacon, Hollis Heimbouch, for her patience, her time, and her poignant interpretations of my narrative. She shined the light on and brought into focus the insights woven between the lines of my manuscript. Our conversations each week enhanced each and every chapter of this book. And to my leopard owl, my beautiful Tess, for her discerning and sensitive questions, her wisdom, her devotion, and her love. She has preciously held my heart every day and night, and most simply put, without her, there would be no book.

ABOUT THE AUTHOR

MAUREEN CHIQUET began her career in marketing at L'Oréal Paris in 1985. She joined The Gap in 1988, first as a merchandise trainee. In 1994 she worked with Jenny Ming to launch Old Navy. In 2002 she became president of Banana Republic, before moving to Chanel in 2003 as chief operating officer and president of US operations. In 2007, she became Chanel's first global chief executive officer, steering it through the 2008 global downturn. Under her leadership, the business grew threefold. Maureen left Chanel in early 2016 to focus on developing new leadership initiatives.

Maureen is a trustee of the Yale Corporation and fellow of Yale University, where she graduated in 1985 with a bachelor of arts in literature. Maureen divides her time between Paris and New York.